Blind Spots, Biases, and Other Pathologies in the Boardroom

Blind Spots, Biases, and Other Pathologies in the Boardroom

Kenneth A. Merchant
Katharina Pick

First published in 2010 by
Business Expert Press, LLC
222 East 46th Street, New York, NY 10017
www.businessexpertpress.com

ISBN-13: 978-1-60649-070-9 (paperback)
ISBN-10: 1-60649-070-2 (paperback)

ISBN-13: 978-1-60649-071-6 (e-book)
ISBN-10: 1-60649-071-0 (e-book)

DOI 10.4128/9781606490716

A publication in the Business Expert Press Corporate Governance collection

Collection ISSN: 1948-0407 (print)
Collection ISSN: 1948-0415 (electronic)

Cover design by Jonathan Pennell
Interior design by Scribe, Inc.

First edition: May 2010

10 9 8 7 6 5 4 3 2 1

Printed in Taiwan

Abstract

Corporate governance is one of the hottest topics in the business world now, as it always is in times of stress. Some of the recently discovered scandals and corporate failures can be traced back to corporate governance failures. Boards of directors must share some of the blame in many of the failures. Something was not working right, even in some boardrooms full of highly qualified individuals.

Boards have been criticized for being too large or too small, for having members who are not independent or who lack the requisite knowledge, or for enabling "bad apple" directors who are inattentive, weak, and even self-serving, among other things. But that is not at all what this book is about. In this book we show how seemingly ideal boards, those with "best practice" size, composition, and structure, can still fail to provide good governance simply because they fall victim to problems inherent in all groups.

While having groups of board members provide corporate oversight is probably necessary, and even advantageous in some respects, groups have a dark side too. Tendencies that occur in group behavior can destroy or obscure the talents of even highly intelligent, energetic, and well-intended individuals, causing collective blind spots, biases, and inefficiencies that can render boards ineffective. Groups often perceive risks differently from the way individual group members do and collectively fail to see problems where they really exist. Groups tend toward conformity in perceptions and attitudes, even when they are obviously wrong. Groups are prone to framing decisions in ways that none of the good decision makers on the board would do individually. And groups often waste time on unimportant details both when more important activities await and when meeting time is severely limited. No group is immune to these destructive patterns, which makes understanding them critically important from a governance standpoint. They can impair board effectiveness even when all the right pieces (and people) are in place.

In this book we argue that as a first step it is important to recognize these group dynamics and the problems they cause. Some of them can be minimized through, for example, properly designed decision processes.

Others are more complicated. But all of them need to be recognized and understood so that we can properly shape our expectations of the degree and quality of oversight corporate boards of directors can provide and so that we can turn our energy toward the many group-level factors that could improve board performance going forward.

This book is intended for board members, managers, and advanced students who want to further their knowledge of boardroom behavior and, particularly, the negative effects that are produced by common boardroom dynamics. The readers of this book will benefit by becoming aware of these potentially serious problems, possible remedies, and trade-offs that must be made.

Keywords

Corporate governance, boards of directors, group dynamics, social psychology, blind spots, biases

Contents

Preface

At first glance, our author team might look a little unusual: a junior organizational behavior professor working with a senior management accounting professor located at a different university. But we did not think it was unusual at all. We are both interested in corporate governance in general and the functioning of boards of directors in particular. For the purpose of studying this topic, our knowledge sets are complementary. The functioning of boards depends crucially on how the board members interact with each other. An organizational behavior professor who specializes in applying social psychology theory to the business world can bring a lot of relevant knowledge to the study of boards. So too can a management accounting professor. Management accounting professors study how managers use information for such purposes as choosing and evaluating business strategies, finding and analyzing problems, and evaluating managers' performances and allocating incentives. These are exactly the kinds of tasks on which board members spend much, if not most, of their time. So our knowledge sets fit together nicely. What we could do together on this project was much better than either of us could have done alone.

In writing this book, we drew on knowledge from multiple sources. We reviewed the research literature on the functioning of groups. While almost none of that knowledge has been developed directly from studies of boards of directors, some of the knowledge that has been developed is clearly applicable to the boardroom setting. We also reviewed the corporate governance literature. While very little of that literature draws directly on findings in social psychology, some of it does discuss problems that board members have in working together. It provides advice and examples that we were able to link back to the research literature. To supplement the theoretical literature, we participated in and observed board meetings in multiple companies. Seeing boards in action was invaluable in helping us to develop the depth of knowledge needed to write this book. We also interviewed many board members. These interviews enabled us to gather anecdotes and insights from a wide range of different industries, companies, and board settings. We proceed from the point of view that boards of directors are fundamentally *groups*, not simple aggregations of individuals. Observations, interviews, and social-psychological theory are, therefore, all essential to understanding how boards work.

We hope and intend that this book provides a nice blend of theory and practice, rigor and relevance. It is not the final word on this subject by any means, because there is so much that is yet to be learned. But we believe that this book provides an accurate, concise summary of what is known about this important topic at this point in time. We hope that many who read the book will be alarmed at the implications and will take steps to ameliorate the problems faced every day by boards and the corporations they serve.

We would be remiss if we did not thankfully acknowledge the many board members who allowed us to interview them or to observe their board meetings. They must remain anonymous, but it is in these meetings that we gathered much of the wisdom and illustrative examples that are contained in this book. We want to acknowledge the helpful suggestions of Kees de Kluyver, Fei Du, Mike Giordano, and Jay Lorsch. And we are indebted to Mason Carpenter, our editor, who has been supportive and helpful from the start.

CHAPTER 1

Oversight by Groups of Board Members

In January 2001, CEO of Tyco International Dennis Kozlowski received an employment contract from his board. Like many CEOs, Kozlowski had served most of his tenure (almost 8 years) without one. However, by 2000 he was asking for a contract. More specifically, he was asking for one that included a clause stating that conviction of a felony was not grounds for termination unless it was materially injurious to the company *and* if "three quarters of the board then voted to oust him."[1]

Although many CEOs have negotiated contracts with generous terms, it was unique to include a felony as something that would not amount to "just cause" for termination. But neither this nor the strange timing of the contract request seemed to catch board members' attention. It is now speculated that the contract was desired only after Kozlowski knew he was under investigation for sales tax evasion.[2]

Four years later, Kozlowski was convicted of misappropriation of hundreds of millions of dollars in corporate funds from Tyco, falsifying business records, and violating business law. He was sentenced to up to 25 years in prison. Tyco, an inspiring tale of free market business success and once the most admired company in America, was for a good portion of the decade a name synonymous with the most egregious examples of corporate greed and fraud.[3]

How could this happen? How could a board of directors approve a contract that removed its power to terminate a CEO even in the case of criminal activity? How could the board of a growing and reputable global conglomerate become so disconnected from its governance role and exhibit such seemingly bad judgment?

The aim of this book is to shine a light on the dynamics and group processes of boards of directors and to describe, particularly, how these dynamics can cause perhaps nearly inevitable failures. These failures will occur even in boards that are seemingly well constructed—for example, of the right size and containing a good mix of highly qualified board members.

The spate of scandals, performance problems, and corporate failures of recent years have caused increasing attention to be focused on boards of directors. This is as it should be. Corporate governance is critically important, and boards of directors are at the heart of the corporate governance process. But the subject of board dynamics and particularly what happens inside the boardroom is almost never explored, largely because the actual board deliberations are seen to be highly sensitive and confidential. But understanding group processes is fundamental to understanding why board failures like Tyco happen. In the following pages, we describe how even "good" boards can develop blind spots, decision-making biases, and other pathologies precisely because boards are—and must operate as—groups.

Corporate governance encompasses the entire set of mechanisms and processes by which business corporations are directed and managed. Good corporate governance helps ensure achievement of long-term objectives, satisfying shareholders and other stakeholders (e.g., creditors, employees, customers, suppliers, local community), while complying with legal and regulatory requirements. It helps corporations create economic value and enhances investor confidence, which is essential for the effective functioning of a market economy.

While there is no single, well-defined, agreed-upon model of good corporate governance, everyone agrees that effectively functioning boards of directors are essential. As observed in one publication of the National Association of Corporate Directors (NACD), boards are "the central mechanism for oversight and accountability in our corporate governance system."[4] They are generally considered the front line of defense. As the duly elected representatives of the shareholders, boards have both the ultimate decision-making authority in the corporation and the ultimate accountability.

Boards are charged with governing the organization through broad policies, objectives, and oversight. Among other things, they play important roles in ensuring that the corporation complies with all laws and regulations; in selecting, appointing, and evaluating the CEO; and in ensuring that resources are acquired and managed effectively and efficiently to guarantee the continuity and success of the organization. The ideal is for boards to challenge managers to strive for high performance, to introduce them to both new business opportunities and contacts, to coach them as necessary, and to hold them accountable. To make this happen, dialogues with management should be open and constructive. Boards should be proactive so as to avoid crises before they happen. Resulting decisions should sometimes be bold, involving significant risk taking, but always carefully considered and implemented.

Because of the central role played by boards of directors, major corporate governance failures, which can be errors of either commission or omission, must be, at least in part, failures of boards of directors. Investors, potential investors, regulators, and indeed all corporate stakeholders are right to be concerned with how boards of directors perform. We have seen that ideal board behavior and performance do not always happen.

Much has been written about board failures, and the identified causes are many. Some boards are too large; others are too small. Some boards have the wrong composition. They contain members who are not independent of management, who lack requisite knowledge, or who have personal conflicts of interest. There are some "bad apple" directors who miss meetings, who are unprepared, inattentive, or both when they do attend, who do not understand the duties and responsibilities of a board member, who are self-serving, or who have the wrong personalities. Some board members are intimidated by management and are too weak to speak up, and conversely, others try to dominate discussions and decision making.

Even with the right composition of members, boards operate with some difficult constraints. The required tasks and legal responsibilities are dauntingly broad and often ambiguous. For example, it is a challenge for board members to maintain the appropriate level of engagement, thereby providing effective oversight without stepping over the "micromanaging" line to meddle in affairs that are best left to management. And boards must rely heavily on management for information, they have little or no direct staff support, and they meet infrequently for only short periods of time.

But these problems of board size, composition, information, timing, and the overall difficulty of the job are not at all what this book is about. In this book we show how seemingly ideal boards, those with "best practice" size, composition, and structure, with enough staff support, and with enough time to consider issues carefully, can *still* fail to provide good governance, simply because they fall victim to some problems inherent in all groups. That is, all groups of individuals who are trying to work together for the common good are subject to some *destructive group dynamics* that cause blind spots, biases, and other decision-making pathologies. Recognizing these problems is a first necessary step. Only then can steps be taken to avoid the problems, or at least to minimize their consequences.

The Power of Groups

In theory, corporate oversight could be provided by an individual, perhaps just a single oversight executive who has authority over the CEO. But even if corporate oversight by a single individual were legally permissible—which it is not—it would not be optimal.

Providing corporate oversight by a *group* of individuals has many advantages. First, it is not wise to grant supreme power to a single individual because it is too easy for that power to be misused. Second, the aggregate knowledge, skills, insights, and business contacts that a board group can apply to the issues at hand are far greater than those possessed by any individual. Third, the combining of ideas in an oversight group tends to minimize the biases and prejudices that might be present in any individual. Unchecked, these biases could be seriously detrimental. And, importantly, where they function well, the value provided by a group is greater than the sum of the values contributed by each of its individual members. Board members who are functioning as a team inform, stimulate, and challenge each other.

Corporate Governance Ideals

What does ideal corporate governance, and board composition and behavior, look like? No general agreement exists, and hard empirical evidence is sparse. But advice abounds. Corporate governance and, more specific for our purposes, board "best practices" have been identified in many articles and books and also by activist investors, including pension funds like California Public Employees' Retirement System and some private investment firms, such as Pershing Square Capital Management. Many ideal board characteristics, and even some sets of best practices intended as largely complete, are also revealed in the evaluation criteria used by a number of outside agencies that rate corporations' governance structures and processes. The most prominent of these agencies are RiskMetrics Group (RMG), which acquired Institutional Shareholder Services (ISS), The Corporate Library (TCL), Audit Integrity, and Governance Metrics International (GMI). Several of these agencies use fairly lengthy lists of best practices to make their ratings. For example, RMG's Corporate Governance Quotient (CGQ) ratings assess firms' governance in eight areas: (a) board structure and composition, (b) audit issues, (c) charter and bylaw provisions, (d) laws of the state of incorporation, (e) executive and director compensation, (f) qualitative factors, (g) director and officer stock ownership, and (h) director education. ISS uses a total of 64 variables both individually and sometimes in combination to develop the CGQ rating. On the other hand, TCL's rating is more subjective and considers just a few factors that are considered to be key indicators.

Research has shown that the differences between some of the ratings are huge; a 2008 study done at Stanford University found that the correlations between the various formal ratings are close to zero.[5] To illustrate the disparity with specifics, recently several major corporations, including General Electric, Pfizer, and Wyeth, were given perfect "100" scores by ISS but given "D" ratings by TCL. Some other companies, including Home Depot, Lockheed Martin, 3M, and Xerox, were given perfect "10" scores by GMI but rated as "F" by TCL.

This same Stanford study also tested the ability of the governance ratings to predict important outcomes such as performance, accounting restatements, and shareholder suits. All the ratings failed this test. The findings revealed all the ratings had weak (i.e., economically trivial) to nonexistent predictive power, except that RMG's ratings had negative predictive power. That is, the firms rated by RMG as being well governed actually had poorer performance indicators—more class action lawsuits, lower return on assets, and lower stock price performance.

These ratings provide numerical illustrations of how far we are from having complete agreement as to what constitutes best corporate governance practice or even an understanding of what leads to effectiveness. Still, there are some micro areas of agreement that provide elements of what will be, eventually, a better developed theory of how to provide effective corporate governance. Some of these areas of agreement relate directly to boardroom practices.

Generally Agreed-Upon Ideals

In this section, taking from all or most of these sources of corporate governance advice, we summarize what we consider to be the most salient, noncontroversial prescriptions regarding board composition, structure, and behavior. We take these prescriptions as a starting point for our discussions. Our presentation here is brief because discussing and analyzing these prescriptions is not our focus. Our main thesis in this book is that even if all these so-called best practices are followed, boards still face some inherent blind spots, biases, and other pathologies that can cause failure.

These are among the boardroom characteristics about which there seems to be general agreement:

1. *Shareholder rights.* The corporate governance structure and processes should protect and facilitate the exercise of shareholder rights. Shareholders should have the right to be sufficiently informed about, and sometimes to participate in or at least express their views about, key corporate decisions. Governance structures and practices should be transparent to shareholders. Insider trading and abusive self-interested behavior should be prohibited. Minority shareholders should be protected from abusive actions of controlling shareholders. Antitakeover devices should not be used to shield management and the board from accountability.

2. *Board member behavior.* Board members should be well informed and act in good faith, with due diligence and care, in the best interest of the company and the shareholders. While directors must necessarily rely on management for information about the company, board members must ensure that they have the requisite information

to develop their own sense of priorities and views. They must devote both the time and attention needed to fulfill their responsibilities.

3. *Board size*. The board of directors should not be too small or too large.[6] Although three is a practical minimum board size, in most cases a board of three members is too small. This is because committees must have three outside board members. Thus, if the entire board includes only three members, every board member would have to be independent, and every board member would have to serve on every board committee, which could mean quite a heavy workload.

Large boards have the potential advantage of including members with varied industry, technical, and leadership expertise, which opens up the possibility for more business opportunities. In addition, the additional resources spread the workload over more people and potentially allow for more detailed discussions of issues.

There is evidence, however, that firms with relatively small boards perform better than firms with very large boards.[7] The larger the board, the more unwieldy it becomes to involve each board member actively in the discussions. Some experts suggest that the optimal board size is perhaps in the range of seven to nine. But the optimal size certainly varies with the size and complexity of the company. For example, because of the need to include some industry experts, a large conglomerate probably needs a larger board than does a smaller firm in a single line of business.

4. *Board composition*. Many characteristics of the individual board members are important. The rule that a majority of the board members must be independent of management and the company is now institutionalized in various government and stock market regulations. In addition, some board members should have specialized expertise, which includes knowledge of the industry and management functions that are important to the company, such as finance, marketing, and logistics. More generally, the board members should be energetic and attentive, traits that are perhaps more likely in directors who are younger and less busy.

5. *Board structure*. Some discussions and decision recommendations should be delegated to committees. Committees tend to comprise

the board members who have the most relevant expertise. Since committees are smaller in size than the full board group, it is easier for all committee members to participate in detailed discussions of issues. Specialized issues can be researched and vetted in the committees, and the committees' recommendations can be approved by the full board. At a minimum, three critical board committees should be established: nominating/governance, audit, and compensation. Other committees can be established, as necessary. The committees should meet regularly and on an additional as-needed basis. To ensure that the full board is properly informed, communication processes between committees and the full board must be effective.

6. *Board leadership.* Management should not have control over the board's agenda. One easy way to ensure that the board controls its own agenda is to have an independent board chair; that is, the roles of CEO and chair can be separated. But some boards maintain control of the agenda by having it set by a "lead outside director." The board should hold regular executive sessions (i.e., without management present), though meeting management is also important. The board should be properly engaged. This requires effective leadership from a leader who uses orderly processes to allow each director to contribute his or her unique talents and perspectives to the issue at hand.

7. *Board focus.* The work of the board should be mostly future oriented. It is tempting for boards to spend a great deal of time on administrative formalities or focused on reviews of financial statements and other reports of what has happened in the past. These are the easy governance tasks. But boards should spend most of their time focused on the future. That is where they add value.

8. *Board evaluations.* The board should evaluate itself regularly. Improvements should be made as necessary. Board membership, structures, and processes should evolve with the needs of the company.

This list of good-practice characteristics is certainly not complete. It does, however, provide a sense of the types of areas that we will *not* be discussing further in this book. We want to proceed by assuming that the board is well constructed and organized so that we can focus on the group decision-making pathologies that can occur in the boardroom *anyway*.

It should be noted that some individual characteristics are not important, at least by themselves; significant differences are and will always be found among boards that are functioning effectively. For example, boards can function effectively with many different operating styles. Some apparently effective boards are quite formal, with meetings in an elaborate boardroom, every board member in business attire, and strict adherence to rules and procedures. Other boards are at the opposite extreme, with meetings held in a more casual setting, board members dressed "comfortably," and discussions more chaotic. Some board meetings are long; others are short. Some board meetings are quite congenial, and others are laden with tension. By themselves these factors are not primary indicators of board success or failure.

The Dark Side of Groups

We now turn to our primary point of interest for this book. Even when most or all the best practices such as those previously described are followed, problems can occur. These problems occur simply because virtually all groups of individuals placed in decision-making roles, even those trying to work together toward a common goal, have an inherently dark side. Natural group tendencies can destroy or obscure the talents even of highly intelligent, energetic, and well-intended individuals, causing collective blind spots, biases, and inefficiencies that can render boards ineffective.

Group biases can cause boards to misperceive risks and fail to see problems where they really exist. Behavioral anchors, social norms, and sometimes inherent natural suppression of dissent can cause groups to tend toward conformity in perceptions and attitudes, even when those perceptions and attitudes are wrong. Groups are prone to framing decisions in ways that none of the good decision makers on the board would individually. And groups often waste time on unimportant details, both when more important activities await and when meeting time is severely limited. These are the subjects of the chapters that follow. No group is immune to these destructive patterns, which makes understanding them critically important from a governance standpoint. These patterns can impair board effectiveness even when all the right pieces (and people) are in place.

As a suggestive example, Enron likely was subject to one or more of the destructive, hidden group blind spots or biases. On paper, Enron's board was seemingly near ideal. It was composed of sophisticated, distinguished industry leaders, as well as widely recognized experts in finance, derivatives, and accounting, each of whom had significant ownership stakes. The board seemed to have an effective structure and ideal board and committee charters and codes of conduct. The board met regularly, the board members were well briefed, the meetings were well organized, and board members uniformly described the internal board relations as "harmonious."[8] But something obviously went very wrong. A U.S. Senate subcommittee concluded, in part, that

> the Enron Board of Directors failed to safeguard Enron sharehold-
> ers and contributed to the collapse of the seventh largest public
> company in the United States, by allowing Enron to engage in
> high risk accounting, inappropriate conflict of interest transac-
> tions, extensive undisclosed off-the-books activities, and excessive
> executive compensation.[9]

Many experts and regulators have considered the Enron situation in general, and the functioning of the Enron board in particular, and have suggested reasons for the eventual failure. Undoubtedly, there were multiple causes of the failure. But while it is difficult to say conclusively, without having observed the board meetings, it seems likely that Enron was subject to one or more of the destructive, hidden forces that are the focus of this book.

The same problems might have existed in other companies that have suffered governance failures. These include major failures such as Tyco, WorldCom, HealthSouth, Adelphia, Fannie Mae, AIG, and Citigroup, and, to emphasize that this is not a problem solely in the United States, also Royal Ahold (Netherlands), Parmalat (Italy), Lernout & Hauspie (Belgium), Hyundai Motor Company (Korea), Ocean Grand Holdings (Hong Kong), China Aviation Oil (Singapore), Guangdong Kelon Electrical Holdings (China), and Satyam (India), just to mention a few. Also included are other smaller corporate governance failures that have resulted in problems, some of which are undoubtedly never detected, such as poor investments, the granting of excessive executive compensation, biased evaluations of management, and misperceptions of risk.

Overview of the Book

In the chapters that follow, we discuss the implications of the reality that boards are not mere aggregations of individuals. They are, for both better and worse, complex social systems. Because the positives of providing corporate oversight through multiperson boards are already widely recognized, we focus on the possible negatives, which are often ignored. We describe what we believe to be the most common blind spots, biases, and other similar pathologies that can be caused by providing corporate governance oversight through *groups* of individuals. We describe each of the pathologies and their possible effects and illustrate their functioning in a real or plausible board situation.

The book is organized as follows: Chapter 2 describes two common ways in which individual behavior changes for the worse in a group setting: *social loafing* and excessive *group conformity*. Chapter 3 discusses two prominent cognitive limitations that occur in group level. One is a *shared information bias*, a tendency for groups to discuss only information that is already shared by all group members rather than exploring novel information. The other is called *pluralistic ignorance*, a systematic underestimation of the degree to which individuals' concerns are shared by others.

Chapter 4 describes *group polarization*, a group tendency to make more extreme, often riskier decisions than its members would individually. Chapter 5 describes *groupthink*, an extreme version of group conformity that also includes some other distinctive and dysfunctional group behaviors. Chapter 6 discusses how *group habitual routines* can entrench behavior even when the behavior is not appropriate for the situations being faced. Chapter 7 explains why *conflict* is inherent in group work and how it can have deleterious effects on group processes and outcomes. Chapter 8 explores the role of *power* in the group setting and how it can be misused. Finally, chapter 9 discusses how working in groups often causes *productivity losses*.

In our concluding chapter, we discuss how to counteract these destructive group dynamics. One challenge in identifying and fixing the harmful group processes we discuss is that many of the processes overlap, and their solutions can be somewhat contradictory. For example, all groups have conformity pressures. But some conformity is good. And not all groups fall victim to groupthink, even though groupthink is a version of conformity. Further, conformity pressures may be reduced by making groups less cohesive; however, reduced group cohesiveness is harmful for *other* reasons. We discuss some inherent boardroom tensions and some difficult trade-offs that must be made. While some of the phenomena we discuss manifest themselves in similar behaviors, the phenomena are conceptually separable. Their causes are different, as are the methods for minimizing their harmful effects.

We proceed from the viewpoint that recognition of the potential problems is the necessary first step. Only then can the effects of some negative group tendencies be avoided or minimized. Some might be addressed somewhat straightforwardly, through, for example, modified board decision processes. Others are perhaps more challenging to deal with. They might require alternate regulatory or administrative devices to prevent the harmful outcomes from occurring.

We have two main goals for this book. First, we wish to provide insights that are useful both for board members and for regulators who are interested in improving corporate governance outcomes. Second, we wish to provide insights that are useful for shaping expectations about the degree and quality of oversight that corporate boards of directors can provide. There are some inherent limitations in what can be expected from oversight provided by groups of board members. Everyone who is relying on the effective functioning of boards of directors needs to understand those limits.

CHAPTER 2

Group Influences on Individual Behavior

Vanessa Roberts walked out of the boardroom frustrated and headed to the restroom to collect her thoughts. She had just confronted fellow director Harry Sykes about his decision to vote—along with the other four directors—to support the proposal to change the compensation metrics for Hayman Inc.'s business unit heads. Vanessa was convinced the reward scheme was not appropriate and would alienate more junior and team-oriented employees. In a professional services firm, she knew this could be costly. Just yesterday, as they discussed the matter on the plane, Harry had agreed with her. Over the course of discussion, however, Harry first seemed uncertain and then ultimately agreed with the other four directors and the CEO in favor of the new plan. This left Vanessa as the lone resister. She was puzzled. How could this happen? Harry was a well-respected, highly competent manager of a thriving company he founded. Yet his resolve seemed weak in this situation.

When Vanessa confronted Harry privately to ask him what changed his mind, he told her that the other directors had pointed out the problems with the current scheme and the potential benefits of changing it. In the course of the discussion, he found himself agreeing with them, and he was now quite certain about his yes vote.

Vanessa knew that the final outcome was uncertain. No one would know the actual consequences of the compensation scheme until it had been in place for some time. Still, she was surprised and confused that Harry was able to change his mind so dramatically and with such conviction.

Vanessa's experience illustrates how operating in a group environment can dramatically influence an individual's beliefs and behaviors. In particular, she saw Harry respond to pressures of conformity that exist in group settings. Even the most competent group members are susceptible to the "power of the group situation."

Groups obviously have certain characteristics or behavioral tendencies that happen at the *collective* level. These will be discussed in the following chapters. This chapter, however, focuses on how *individual* behavior is shaped by group settings. Because people draw information about themselves from the groups to which they belong, groups exert a great deal of influence over individual beliefs, perceptions, and behaviors. In this chapter, we discuss two ways in which people behave differently in groups than they do individually: through social loafing and through conformity as described in the vignette at the beginning of the chapter. Each of these two phenomena is critically important when we consider board outcomes, and both draw attention to ways in which we can help boards benefit from the diverse and accomplished individuals they assemble to govern.

Social Loafing

One of the great puzzles of board failures is always how the highly accomplished and respected people who compose most boards could appear to have been simply inattentive, disengaged, or disinterested in the performance of their director duties. Certainly there are many angles from which to approach this question, including citing the ways in which directors may be overwhelmed by what is expected of them, unclear about their roles, or simply involved in a flawed process. However, one truth is that most boards are probably getting less effort out of their individual directors than they would if those directors were hired individually as, say, consultants whose job it was to provide governance oversight. This is true because of what psychologists call "social loafing." It is the tendency for individuals to reduce the effort they put into a task when they are working as part of a group as opposed to working alone.[1]

Social loafing was first recorded by German researcher Max Ringelmann, who asked workers to pull on a rope as hard as they could, first individually and then as part of a group with seven other individuals.[2] Ringelmann found that workers pulled harder on the rope when they did it individually than when they were pulling as part of a team. Although groups obviously produce greater total pulling power than any single individual could alone, the total power was lower than what was theoretically expected of the group. In other words, the whole was less than the theoretical sum of its parts.

Social loafing is distinct from productivity losses that result from coordination problems. Coordination loss results if people simply are having difficulty coordinating their effort, perhaps by resting and pulling on the rope at different times, and therefore the total effort cannot capture the full cumulative value of all the individual efforts. A follow-up experiment to Ringelmann's demonstrated that whereas some coordination loss does happen, a significant part of what he observed was indeed a reduction of effort on the part of the individuals.[3]

Since that time, the finding has been replicated many times over, on a variety of different tasks. We now know that social loafing happens, not just in physical tasks, like rope pulling, cheering, and clapping, but also in creative tasks (idea generation) and perceptual, evaluative, and cognitive tasks. It also does not matter whether the task's aim is to maximize some kind of performance or to optimize, or whether the task is additive or one in which individual contributions are averaged to some group score. The phenomenon also happens across gender, age, and culture, although there are variations in the degree to which it happens.[4]

Social loafing shares a common thread with what economists and game theorists call the "free rider" problem, where individuals shirk in contributing to a social good but still benefit from the fact that others contribute.[5] The two concepts are similar because both involve a decrease in motivation when there is a group of others also contributing. However, social loafing has other roots as well, so it must not be treated as interchangeable with the free rider problem.

It is not difficult to see why social loafing could be problematic for boards. Much of what boards do—including preparing for meetings, discussing matters with and questioning management, evaluating strategic plans, and making important decisions—is collective. The board members are not simply working side by side; they are working on a collective, interdependent task, for which the group together will be accountable. A large portion of the information we have about boards is about the individual directors who serve, and our expectations of boards center on what we know of these individuals and the accomplishments, experience, and work they have outside of the board. If directors, in some way, bring less effort or engagement than we would assume given their backgrounds, their success, and the individual positions they hold professionally, boards clearly are losing a major perceived benefit of having assembled the group in the first place. Most important, though, from the perspective of any board that is looking for the best effort from its members and to avoid unnecessary deficiencies, it is essential to understand when and why loafing occurs and how it can be avoided.

Theory and Evidence

When does social loafing occur, and what can we do about it? It appears that people are most likely to loaf when they believe their individual effort will not be visible and identifiable to others, when they believe their effort will not necessarily affect the group performance on a task, and when the task itself has little meaning or significance for them. Finally, there is some evidence that individuals adjust their effort according to what kind of effort they expect others in the group to exert.

Identifiability

Individuals are believed to loaf in groups in part because their efforts are not easily identified by others. Board members, like all individuals, generally want to be evaluated positively by others, especially by other members of a group that is important to them. However, at times they likely feel that a poor individual effort from them would not be visible in the group's work, making it safe not to try very hard. On the flip side, board members might feel that *good* performance on their part would not be recognized but rather would simply blend with the group's overall performance. This lack of potential for a distinct individual evaluation is what can lead to lower motivation for individuals in groups.

Many psychologists believe that simply creating evaluation possibilities for the individual inputs that people offer in a collective activity could eliminate almost all social loafing.[6] But in many group settings, including most work of boards of directors, this is very difficult to do.

Impact or Dispensability of Effort

We must add to this discussion the question of whether or not the individual board members believe their effort will actually matter to the performance or outcome of the group. When people believe that their group task will be accomplished regardless of their effort, they are more inclined to "free ride," as discussed previously, particularly if they have no other intrinsic reason for being engaged with the task.[7] Individuals may perceive that their effort is dispensable, but they can also consider it to be redundant. In other words, when people believe they make no unique contribution to the outcome of the group, they become less motivated and more inclined to loaf.

An extension of this, as Hardy and Crace have found, is that unskilled group members are more likely to loaf than skilled ones.[8] In the boardroom, then, it is conceivable that less experienced directors, or those with less direct expertise in a particular area, may be more inclined to loaf, when they have the opportunity to blend into the crowd.

Importance of the Task

Both factors just described are contingent on the question of whether or not the task itself is meaningful to the individual. When people care about the task itself, they are more likely to exert the kind of effort that they would exert individually.[9] It is important to note, though, that whether or not a task is meaningful can be shaped by many different things. Some tasks may be intrinsically interesting, important, or both to some people. Other tasks may become important because they are highly valued by the group, and by putting effort into the task, the individual gets approval and acceptance from an identity group that is important to that individual. Still other tasks may be important to the individual because he or she truly values the collective success of the group. This is where researchers have found differences, both between cultures and between men and women. Women and people in Eastern cultures, which tend to value intrinsically the performance and well-being of the collective more than do their counterparts (men and people in most Western cultures), tend to exhibit lower levels of loafing.[10]

One might argue that board members obviously perceive their tasks as extremely important and so are highly motivated to perform them and that this should overcome any tendency to loaf. However, this kind of blanket argument overlooks some of the more tedious and repetitive tasks involved in board work. It also fails to acknowledge that boards often have numerous discussions around a particular topic, revisiting concerns, getting consensus, and working through ambiguous issues. All these processes may be long and arduous. It is not always easy to identify the part of any one task that may be "important" or the one that will lead to a particular desired outcome.

Social Loafing on Boards

As is evident from the theory previously described, social loafing does not occur simply in flawed, lazy individuals who are looking for a free ride. All it requires is people who are working on a task as a group rather than individually.

How can we keep boards from losing valuable individual contributions through the effects of social loafing? When we consider how social loafing plays out in the board room, we must think about the various collective tasks that are involved in board work. Social loafing is most likely to occur on those tasks in which directors truly feel they are acting as a collective, rather than simply doing work side by side, and on tasks not seen as intrinsically motivating or important.

For some directors, the preparation of board materials may seem like an individual task, one that is done alongside the other board members. However, when directors come to the meeting and collectively listen to, engage with, and question management in order to draw out and evaluate information, the task quickly becomes a collective one. In other words, they are dependent on each other for the collective outcome of the group, whether or not they draw out the right information and whether or not they can effectively evaluate what is going on. Tasks like evaluating the CEO, setting compensation, and approving important strategic decisions are even more obviously collective ones. These tasks may become particularly vulnerable to loafing when board members do not see them either as important or as intrinsically motivating.[11] This may depend on how tasks are framed for the board, whether or not the board members perceive themselves over time as having an impact on the company, and how seriously tasks have been taken in the past.

Consider the following example of the board of a financial services company. Although the company itself had a clear mission to serve a particular community of clients, individual directors were unclear about either what unique qualifications they brought to the board or what their roles were. The 12 members of this relatively large board were selected primarily in order to bring legitimacy, status, and community connections to the board. In spite of being accomplished professionals, many of the directors simply did not have a clear sense of contributing anything uniquely to the actual work of the board. Some expressed feeling redundant, and most felt they were dispensable. None were able to articulate a clear contribution that was expected of them to the direction of the company.

Although we cannot draw direct causal conclusions here, this board showed many signs of disengagement. In the meeting it was obvious that some directors were reading the board materials for the first time. Most also did not participate actively in discussion or information sharing. In the interviews it became clear that several directors were unprepared for the discussions, could not recall an important issue that had been discussed at great length at a previous meeting, and also did not express positions on issues that had come up at the most recent meeting. Some directors even expressed frustration with others who they claimed were perpetually unprepared or disinterested. One director put it this way:

> The other board members never express any concerns. Unfortunately in most cases people leave board meetings and just put their notes in a drawer, or throw them away, or show up at the next meeting and say, "OK what did we do last time? Let's look at the notes." That's the way it is.

At some level, the disengagement had become visible and conscious, at least to some board members. Outside of the boardroom, these directors were highly respected CEOs, physicians, and community leaders—in other words, not the kind of people one might expect to be disengaged from important governance tasks.

Stories like this can serve as little more than illustrative anecdotes since social loafing is not easily isolated without a true experimental design. But the conditions for it were rife on this board. Of course, social loafing does not have to be, and typically is not, this visible. In fact, it typically occurs unnoticed, probably even to those who are engaged in it.

Ways to Minimize Social Loafing

What can boards do to minimize social loafing? As alluded to in the previous example, one important goal for boards should be that individual directors believe that their contributions are unique and will be observable. Part of this can be achieved in how directors are selected and in how they are interviewed and oriented to their membership.

Great point! — Another component is how the discussions are structured. Do board members really expect to participate? Recent research suggests that one tactic board leaders can use to get buy-in and meaningful engagement from the whole director group is periodically to poll the board, asking each director to offer input to a point of discussion.[12]

Doing more work in committees is another way in which loafing may be reduced. The smaller the group, the less anonymous the members and the more the individuals believe they will have an impact on the group outcome. Even aside from the standing committees of the board, it is possible to create temporary committees to take on particular strategic issues or other matters. Some boards we observed used temporary committees to address sporadic activities or short-term business issues, like considering a specific new market or managing a particular relationship important to the company. For example, one board whose company was considering moving its largest office to a new building relied on three directors to work especially closely with management in evaluating the various prospects and working out the important relationships. Directors who agreed to help on this kind of temporary committee were then more directly responsible for an aspect of the board's business. It was a different way of sharing the work and a way that created greater accountability and also greater engagement from those who were directly involved.

Finally, and perhaps most obviously, directors should be individually evaluated. In order for evaluation potential and identifiability to matter in a group setting, an evaluation standard must exist.[13] This means that director roles and expectations must be spelled out and rigorously and meaningfully evaluated, preferably by the rest of the board and also by board leadership.

Pressure Toward Conformity

Another aspect of group influence that can alter individual behavior and perception is the pressure toward conformity that happens when people are in the presence of others. Certainly, when we consider some of the great governance failures of the current time, we wonder whether individual directors considered pushing against the tide in the boardroom when they were either outnumbered or simply unsure of a particular course of action. When the Enron board approved the financial statements or the dismissal of the ethics guidelines, were there some individuals in the room who were uncertain or who even doubted the decision but did not speak up? Post hoc accounts and even testimonies suggest that the answer to this question is yes.

The Conformity Concept

Psychological research on conformity shows that groups are enormously powerful environments when it comes to shaping the behaviors and even the beliefs of individual group members. This is true in part because members of groups often assume that they are similar to other group members and that they share common beliefs, even when the group is randomly assembled and there is no reason for the individuals to have similar beliefs. Group members' beliefs sometimes conform not simply by the group situation but by attribution that the individuals in the group make about the others in the group.

Psychologists distinguish between two types of conformity.[14] *Normative conformity* occurs when an individual revises what he or she claims to believe in order to go along with the group but privately believes something different. *Informational conformity*, on the other hand, occurs when an individual actually revises his or her own privately held belief. The feature that distinguishes these two types of conformity is the motive for conforming. Normative conformity happens because people want to be accepted by the group in order to reap positive social rewards. Informational conformity happens because people are looking to improve their judgment or inform their beliefs by relying on some set of trusted others— when they see others as sources of information. Although we can distinguish these two types of conformity conceptually, in most real-world situations they are both present and difficult to isolate.[15]

Theory and Evidence

The power of conformity pressures was most famously illustrated by Muzafer Sherif[16] and Solomon Asch[17] in their respective experiments involving two tasks of perception. Sherif asked his subjects to estimate whether and how much a pinpoint of light, shone in a dark room, was moving. This was designed to be an ambiguous task, since under these conditions the light often appears to be moving even though it is not (known as the autokinetic effect). The real point, however, is that subjects were consistently affected by the judgments of those around them. First, subjects were asked individually to estimate the amount of movement. When asked again in groups of three, subjects tended over a series of trials to revise their own judgments and converge as a group around a central number. Subjects were typically not aware that they had been influenced, denying that those around them had affected their judgments in any way. Interestingly, when asked to estimate the movement distance alone again, in yet another round, they held onto the new revised judgments.

Asch's experiment required subjects to match the length of a line with one of three other lines, two of which were obviously unequal. Before each subject gave his or her answer, seven other supposed members of the group, who were actually cooperating with Asch, unanimously provided what was clearly the wrong response. Under this influence, one third of the subjects agreed with the seven, providing incorrect answers in an objective and easy task. Together these experiments illustrate that conformity happens not only in situations where information is ambiguous but also in situations where the "correct" answer is easily identifiable and individuals are in a good position to make their own, independent judgments.

The experiments also reveal some important distinctions in how conformity can work. Asch was able to identify among his conforming subjects three categories: those who truly adopted a new judgment and were not aware that they had been influenced, those who thought they saw something different but began to doubt it when the majority disagreed, and finally those who knew their judgment was correct but simply chose to go along with the majority in order not to "appear different from or inferior to others."[18] Note that subjects in all these categories would still *behave* in conformity with the group.

When we consider what conditions make the pressures for conformity more or less powerful, several important factors emerge. First, as suggested above, people are more susceptible to conformity pressures when situations are unclear and ambiguous. Second, people are more easily influenced when they believe that the group around them is highly competent and credible. High-status people tend to induce more conformity to their perceptions and judgments than do low-status people. And finally, a person's own characteristics can make him or her more or less susceptible. Whether it is an enduring trait or it arises only briefly in the moment, how qualified or capable a person *feels* in a situation shapes how much they will rely on those around them for beliefs and judgments. Someone who has consistently high self-confidence therefore would be less susceptible than someone who does not. Of course, confidence and perceived qualifications can rise and fall in the moment as well.

In addition to these, the larger the majority that expresses a certain belief, the more conformity, both information and normative, will follow. This effect levels off at about six people, beyond which additional people make little added difference. Another critical factor is unanimity. In Asch's study, it was crucial that all seven people expressed the *same* wrong opinion. Even someone stating a different *wrong* answer decreases conformity, making the target individual more willing and able to stake a stand against a group where someone has already expressed a difference from the majority. In Asch's study, one other person providing a deviant answer, even an incorrect one, made conformity drop from 32% to 6%.

One might rightfully question whether these pressures would still hold true when the task at hand is more significant than estimating the length of a line. An experiment involving a police lineup showed that, when subjects perceived the task to be more important, the influence toward conformity was even greater.[19]

Conformity and the conditions under which it is most powerful may be quite intuitive. However, we often overlook how powerful it can be, particularly in situations where we assume individuals are independent, competent, and self-confident.

Conformity on Boards

Unfortunately, conformity pressures are particularly high in board settings. Most information and decisions that confront boards are unclear and ambiguous. For the most part, directors tend to hold those around them in high regard, or at least are keenly aware of each other's professional status and accomplishment. Finally, there are moments in board meetings when directors feel wholly unqualified or relatively outclassed in terms of evaluating a particular decision or discussion point. When directors open up about their experiences, it is obvious that they doubt themselves at times.

What is the problem with conformity in the boardroom? First, as seen in the experiments described previously, the group can actually come to a conclusion or belief that is wrong, despite the fact that some people in the group have the correct answer, simply because the latter are outnumbered. This is the most obvious problem. However, conformity also limits the potential capabilities of the group in other ways. Researchers have illustrated that groups in which a minority opinion is simply *expressed* engage in more innovative and careful thinking, often leading to better decision making and more creative solutions. Given the power of majority influence in preventing such minority viewpoints even from being heard, we can see how boards may fail to get the benefits of diversity they hope to get.

Finally, conformity has importance not only in regard to specific tasks but also in the behavioral norms that are formed in the group. Groups form strong norms particularly around behaviors most relevant to the group's survival and work, and they tend to conform around the kinds of behaviors that are rewarded versus punished by the group itself and also by the group's environment. On a board, one could imagine, for example, pressures around how and when one should speak up or criticize in meetings. Subtle pressures can lead directors simply to adopt the expected behaviors rather than challenge what seems to be the uniformly accepted way of doing things. On boards this may be particularly powerful because membership rotates rarely and typically people are added to the board one by one, meaning at any point in time the new person is joining an already well-established group and observable set of behaviors.

Consider a board like the one we observed. This board of an industrial equipment supply company had seven members who had an average tenure of 11 years: longer than most boards. This extended tenure perhaps exaggerates our point, but it makes it nonetheless. The board had adopted a style of operating that involved little discussion among the directors. Most of the board meeting airtime was taken by the CEO. Interruptions and criticisms were usually met with disdain both from the CEO and from other directors. Although tension was palpable in the meeting, the directors had adopted a genteel, nonconfrontational way of communicating and taking in information. Most meaningful discussion in fact occurred outside of the main board meeting. One director who had a great deal of experience and stature both in the industry and with other large, prestigious boards was added to this board. He came to this particular board culture attempting to contribute with critical questions and thoughts; however, he was quickly silenced. He began to keep his ideas to himself. After less than one full term on the board, he decided to remove himself, asking continually for the board to seek a replacement for him. This particular director had the level of experience and self-assurance that enabled him to decide simply to step off the board. This is always within a director's set of options; however, depending on the perceived relative status of board members and on the importance of a particular board membership to a director's concept of self, it may be either more or less difficult to step off versus simply conforming to the board's style.

Pushing Back Against Conformity

What can boards do to minimize the negative effects of conformity? Unfortunately, conformity pressures are an inherent problem due to the social nature of board work. However, if it is acknowledged how deeply ingrained conformity is in group behavior and human nature, boards may be able to guard against at least its detrimental effects.

For example, boards can make dissent a regularly occurring and accepted event in board discussion. Some boards regularly assign an individual or subset of directors to act as devil's advocate during important discussions. This is different from *true* dissent, where an individual risks alienation from the group. But it can keep boards hearing a minority opinion and open up creative avenues for problem solving and decision making. More broadly than this, however, the way dissent is responded to in the boardroom, by other directors and particularly by board leadership, can critically shape how much risk directors perceive when they hold a viewpoint different from that of the majority of the group. Boards must create conditions where dissent is expected, not just accepted, by the group.

It has been found that social cohesiveness can increase conformity pressures. While cohesiveness is likely an important component to effective performance, boards can make an effort to create high cohesiveness around their tasks but not around strong social ties. It will become evident in this book that many attributes that are detrimental to group process are also beneficial. Cohesiveness is one of these. Groups that are more socially cohesive may be more likely to voice dissent or to deal with dissent constructively than are groups that are less cohesive. For example, when conflict occurs, individuals may be less likely to interpret disagreement as an attack or as emotionally loaded, since they have strong social cohesion with other members. This will become relevant in chapter 7 on group conflict. However, as we consider conformity pressures here, it is important to highlight the distinctly negative role social cohesiveness can play. Social cohesiveness can make individuals more dependent on group approval and acceptance and, in the extreme, can lead to a crippling phenomenon of conformity called "groupthink," which will be covered later in this book.

Boards may also decide periodically to reflect on the process and the assumptions they have as a group, in order to surface norms that may have become ingrained in the way the group actually functions. Boards likely have strong norms about speaking up and expressing dissent, sharing airtime among directors and with management, and the approach taken to to conflict; they also have beliefs about the environment from which the board feels pressure. Unless boards are deliberate about the norms they create, the natural tendency, as with any group, will be toward uniformity and toward norms that promote conformity. As illustrated previously, this not only may leave the board assuming correctness when in fact they have collectively come to a wrong conclusion but also can keep the board from benefiting from diversity of opinion and creative thinking. *very important point!*

CHAPTER 3

Group Cognitive Limitations

Rebecca Halloran, director at Chantech Inc., leaned back in her seat as Larry called for a motion to approve the proposal for development of a new product line the directors had been discussing for the last 45 minutes. She felt the board had had a thorough discussion and thus was pleased and comfortable with the unanimous yes vote that was about to take place. From the very start, the directors had appeared to be on the same page. Most of the concerns and ideas offered by the others had also occurred to Rebecca before the meeting, which only confirmed to her that they were all on the right track. Hal and Jim offered important information from a recent, highly publicized product launch that supported Chantech's proposed move. Rebecca and the others, familiar with the launch, nodded knowingly at the connection that Hal and Jim had articulated between this product and the current discussion.

Frank, who had more direct experience than the other directors with the niche medical product industry they were entering, reflected back what others were already saying. Because of his expertise, this was reassuring both to Rebecca and evidently also to the other directors. The discussion continued for nearly an hour simply because the directors wanted to be sure they had considered all the relevant information and had allowed everyone to articulate their ideas. Satisfied that they had considered all aspects of the matter, they turned to the vote and, indeed, the proposal was approved unanimously.

The board decision illustrated here shows how boards can have what seems to be an open, thorough, and lengthy decision-making process, where directors are comfortable with both process and outcome precisely because they are sharing only information about which they already agree and with which they are already familiar. It is an instance of a group-level cognitive limitation called the *shared information bias*.

Cognitive limitations have adverse effects on any decision made by a board of directors. Some of these limitations are in the cognitive abilities of each individual board member. People have inherent limitations in, for example, their memories and information processing capabilities. Having decisions made by a group of individuals can minimize some of the effects of these limitations. But interestingly, some cognitive limitations persist even when individuals are placed in a group decision-making setting, and some limitations even become more salient. In this chapter we identify some of the most important individual cognitive limitations. However, our primary focus is on two of the most common, and most significant, cognitive limitations that appear only in group decision-making settings: the shared information bias and pluralistic ignorance.

Individuals' Cognitive Limitations

Even the very intelligent, motivated, and experienced members of well-constructed boards have limits in their perceptual, recollection, information processing, and reasoning abilities.[1] All individuals make mistakes caused by, for example, failures in abilities to learn from experience in understanding the world. Individuals focus excessively on information that is readily available or recent. Individuals tend to overestimate what they know. Individuals tend to be overly comforted by the status quo, which leads them to ignore information that is inconsistent with their current beliefs and to do what is comfortable rather than what is important. Individuals have a very limited working memory capacity, both for storing information and for manipulating information. And individuals are quite good at retrieving information quickly from a large knowledge base, but they have relatively little computational power. As a consequence, their reasoning is heavily biased toward using knowledge rather than computation, and they often use heuristics that simplify the issues inappropriately.

These human limitations are well known, and they have been known for a long time. Consequently, social structures and decision support systems have been designed and implemented to magnify individuals' abilities and minimize their failings. Indeed, providing corporate over-sight by a board group rather than a single individual is intended, in part, to expand the pool of cognitive abilities applied to the oversight function. These cognitive biases exist in even the smartest, most talented individuals, and they persist even when individuals are placed in a group setting where decision processes can be designed to reduce the effect of the biases. Consider remedies to the *confirmation bias*—the tendency for all individuals to consider information that confirms one's initial prefer-ences while ignoring disconfirming information. Where the confirmation bias is seen to be a particularly salient problem, decision processes can be designed to ban any public statements of initial preferences, include a full range of information in the board package, and include people with divergent backgrounds and views on the board and allow and encourage them to express their opinions.

As another example, consider what might be done to minimize the *sunk cost bias*—the tendency to "honor" already spent resources that should be deemed irrelevant in making go or no-go decisions. This bias has been identified as contributing to numerous major project fail-ures, all of which required the involvement and concurrence of boards of directors, including Euro Disney, the Millennium Dome in London, the Denver International Airport, and the development of the Concorde supersonic passenger airliner.[2] In fact, the sunk cost bias is also some-times referred to as the "Concorde Effect" because that example is so well known and so representative of the bias. Even after it became appar-ent that the Concorde would not generate enough revenues to become profitable, the British and French governments continued to fund the joint development of the airplane.[3] The flawed logic in all of these cases is that discontinuing the project would be a waste of the resources that had already been spent. The sunk cost bias can be minimized (but not elimi-nated) by the use of decision aids that keep the focus on future cash flows and returns, by training people "not to throw good money after bad," and by creating a culture that supports admissions of mistakes.

Group-Caused Cognitive Limitations

The cognitive limitations of the individuals in the group may or may not be ameliorated by the group's composition or decision processes. Our concern here is that having decisions made by groups of people actually creates some additional biases. Two of these biases appear to be the most common and most potentially important: the shared information bias and pluralistic ignorance.

The Shared Information Bias

It is well known that groups of individuals can pool their individual knowledge and expertise to take advantage of far more information than is available to any single individual. That is a huge advantage of group decision making. However, it is also well documented that in discussions, groups tend to spend too much time examining information that many group members know in common—so-called *shared information*—rather than information known to one or only a few group members—*unshared information*. This decision-process pathology is the *shared information bias*, which is also sometimes referred to as the *hidden profile effect*. It is a pervasive phenomenon and has been replicated in many research studies.[4]

The effect of the shared information bias is simple—flawed decision outcomes. Consideration of the unshared information—*hidden profiles*—might lead to a totally different conclusion. The importance of the bias will vary directly with the importance of the consequences of the decision being considered. In some cases, the effects of the bias might be immaterial. In other cases, they could be catastrophic.

The bias toward shared information has several causes. First, because more people have access to shared information, by definition, the chances that at least some of the elements of the shared information will be mentioned by at least someone in the group decision-making setting is higher.

Second, the bias arises because group discussions serve two quite different purposes. Discussions allow groups to share information that might influence a decision. This can be called the *informational influence* of discussions. But discussions also give individual group members the opportunity to influence each other's opinions on the issue. This is the *normative influence*. Discussing unshared information might be enlightening to the group, but this information is less likely to provoke heated responses, or even to be repeated or reconsidered during discussion. On the other hand, discussing shared information is much more likely to make the group feel it is working toward a consensus. Not surprisingly, then, the potential for the shared information bias is higher when groups are motivated more to reach decision closure than to make the best possible decision.[5]

Third, the shared information bias exists because the final judgments of individual group members seem to be largely predetermined, as we mentioned previously. Most people argue in favor of their own personal preferences and resist changing their minds. Shared information, which is seen as more valid and reliable precisely because it is shared, is more likely to be seen as diagnostic. The judgments of individual group members are often not greatly affected by new pieces of information that surface during the group discussions unless something unusual happens to highlight the importance of that new information. That highlighting of importance is less likely with unshared information that is not repeated and reconsidered in the discussions.

Finally, the shared information bias is prevalent because in many group decision-making settings the desire to maintain harmonious relations with fellow group members is greater than the desire to explore all decision aspects. Individuals prefer both to offer and to receive shared information than they do unshared information, and they judge others who are offering shared information as more credible, knowledgeable, and competent.[6] Not surprisingly, then, group members implicitly focus on information that they know others also possess instead of trying to focus attention on information that only they possess.

Shared information biases have been shown to be significant in many experimental settings. One series of studies found that only 18% of unshared relevant information (i.e., that known only to one group member) was mentioned in group discussions. In contrast, an average of 46% of shared information was discussed, which is more than a 2:1 consideration ratio.[7]

Might we expect that the shared information bias is also common in corporate boardrooms? The answer to this question is almost certainly yes. The bias is less likely if group members have a clear expectation that their decision problem has a certifiably correct answer.[8] But that almost never exists in a boardroom situation. Low group member confidence contributes to the concurrence seeking that tends to occur during group discussions.

How might this bias be weakened? Interestingly, providing explicit instructions for group members to try to uncover as much information as possible and to explore fully all decision alternatives does not seem to eliminate the bias.[9] But other remedies can be effective:

1. *Altering group composition.* More experienced group members are more likely to avoid the tendency to ignore unshared information and often intervene to focus the group's attention on unshared information.[10]

2. *Extending the time available for discussion.* Groups tend to discuss shared information first. They are more likely to consider unshared information in longer meetings.[11]

3. *Assigning one member the role of devil's advocate.* This requires being alert for the introduction of unshared information and advocacy.

4. *Using group decision support systems.* Some decision support systems give decision-making groups access to an array of tools that might alleviate the shared information bias. These tools could include databases, search engines, group communication protocols and aids, and computational tools. Boards can use technology to structure processes for information search and retrieval, group communication, and decision making (e.g., voting). For example, one study showed that groups that were forced to "meet" only via computer were significantly more likely to avoid the shared information bias than were groups that met face to face.[12]

Pluralistic Ignorance

In 2007, before the meltdown of the home-building industry, the CEO of Johnson Homes Inc. (JHI), a publicly traded regional home builder with nearly $2 billion in annual sales, presented his plan to have JHI adopt a new enterprise resource planning (ERP) system built on the Oracle platform. A researcher learned later that many of the board members were uncomfortable in that meeting. The costs of the ERP implementation were significant. The total expected out-of-pocket costs were estimated at slightly over $30 million, and there would be other difficult-to-quantify costs of personnel time and of disruptions of operations and risks of failure.

Many of the individual board members knew that ERP implementation failures were common, as ERP failures in some prominent organizations, including Hershey, Nike, and Whirlpool, had gotten considerable publicity. And the timing for this project was questionable. The medium-term sales forecasts for the home-building industry were uncertain. Some economists were predicting a sizable slowdown for the industry. But none of the JHI board members expressed any reservations about this information technology investment. They all assumed that their fellow board members supported the proposal, so they did not speak up. The proposed investment was approved with but minimal discussion.

Not long after the project began, JHI revenues fell precipitously. By the spring of 2008, monthly revenues were running 70% below those of the comparable month in 2007. The ERP effort had to be abandoned.

One plausible interpretation of this example is as an illustration of a group decision-making pathology called *pluralistic ignorance*. Pluralistic ignorance exists where members of a group hold varied opinions or beliefs but do not express them in the mistaken belief that they are inconsistent with the opinions of others in the group. Pluralistic ignorance prompts people to conform to group norms that do not exist, except in their own confused minds. It stems from natural human tendencies both to overestimate the extent to which their views diverge from group norms and to want to be seen as a cooperative member of the group.

While the pluralistic ignorance concept had been identified and studied earlier, the concept was popularized in 2001 by one writer's description of what he called the "Abilene paradox."[13] He explained his family's decision to continue on a trip to Abilene even though every member of the family had private reservations about the trip. He wrote,

Here we were, four sensible people who . . . had taken a 106-mile trip across a godforsaken desert in a furnace-like temperature through a cloud-like dust storm to eat unpalatable food at a hole-in-the-wall cafeteria in Abilene, when none of us had really wanted to go.[14]

Because the biases of individual group members are interdependent, pluralistic ignorance is defined at the group level as the extent to which group members underestimate the degree to which others share their concerns.[15] Pluralistic ignorance can occur in many different kinds of group settings, including board meetings, and the problems it causes can be significant. It leads to what has been called a *spiral of silence* in which a reluctance to speak out increases the tendency for group members to underestimate the extent to which their concerns are shared with other group members, which further increases the reluctance to speak out. The effect of the problem is that groups follow norms, policies, or practices and make decisions with which most individual group members privately disagree.[16]

While pluralistic ignorance is a pervasive problem that can occur in virtually every kind of group decision-making setting, several preconditions make it more likely to occur. One precondition is when individuals in the group are reluctant to express minority opinions. This is a common tendency to which we have already referred. It might be attenuated by such factors as board member personalities and board culture, but the general tendency is endemic to the group setting. Everyone wants to be liked. There is considerable evidence that those who express minority opinions are more likely to be evaluated unfavorably by the other group members and are more likely to experience *social distancing*. Those who experience social distancing lose social status, they are less likely to have their opinions valued, and they might be excluded from group social events.

Although pluralistic ignorance has not been studied much in the boardroom, almost assuredly it exists there. One study did find it to be a significant determinant of the commonly observed problem of *strategic persistence*.[17] Strategic persistence involves the continuation of a business strategy even in the face of poor business performance.

The pluralistic ignorance problem can be addressed in three important and related ways:

1. The board leadership must maintain a culture that encourages open communication and, particularly, open dissent. Board members must be expected to ask critical questions about the information and decision proposals presented by management. No subject should be undiscussable. Dissent should be treated as a board member obligation. The culture of open dissent is easier to encourage with a diverse board and one with minimal social ties.[18]

2. The pluralistic ignorance problem might be attenuated where there is significant board member turnover. Over time, people get socialized into fixed sets of belief systems. New board members provide a potential to introduce new ideas, to ask new and different questions, and to shake up the status quo.

3. Somewhat contradictorily, the pluralistic ignorance problem is less likely to be faced where board diversity is low and where social cohesion is high. Diversity, particularly with respect to educational and functional backgrounds and gender, tends to exacerbate the pluralistic ignorance problem.[19] On diverse boards, the board members are less likely both to understand each other's positions well and to have the courage to speak up.

Conclusion

In this chapter we discussed some of the prominent cognitive limitations inherent in individual and group decision-making processes. These limitations cause biases and errors in the judgments made in corporate boardrooms. The effects of these limitations can be reduced by the use of decision aids, well-designed decision processes, board composition, and training. But they cannot be eliminated. Boards must be constantly aware of their limitations and biases and guard against their deleterious effects.

CHAPTER 4

Group Polarization

Tom Newberg, chairman of the board of Plaxicor, decided after a generous break for lunch to call the directors back to the board table. They still had one very important strategic matter to cover, and it needed to get adequate attention before directors started zoning out or thinking ahead to catching their flights. It was the decision to acquire Alitec, a small local company whose yet uncertain but potentially groundbreaking technology for storing blood could get Plaxicor's newest product to market almost 2 quarters early, give them a huge step up on competitors, and potentially give them exclusive access to the technology that competitors would soon rely on as well. Tom had prepared for the discussion and asked each director to let him know in advance which of four options he or she favored: (a) an outright acquisition, which had been described in management's reports to be the most risky option; (b) a partnership with Alitec, which was slightly less risky; (c) an exclusive contract that would lock in a price and materials for Plaxicor, which was even less risky; or finally (d) simply to wait for Alitec to come through with the technology, the least risky of the options.

From the looks of it, his directors were feeling skeptical about whether Alitec would indeed succeed with their new technology and thought it unwise to bet too much on it by acquiring them. Three of the seven had said they would support a partnership. Two had preferred the even safer exclusive contract option. Only two had said they would opt for an all-out acquisition. Tom's sense was that directors would easily gather around what seemed like a central position to partner with Alitec. Staying largely out of the discussion himself, he was surprised that his directors settled after only a short time on pursuing the acquisition. He was not

sure whether to interject and remind directors of their own private concerns that they had sent to him. But the group seemed
comfortable with its decision and excited about the prospects.
Their vote was unanimous, and Tom, befuddled but encouraged,
decided to move on with the agenda.

Great point!

One intriguing and often beguiling facet of group behavior is that collective decision making does not always produce a better outcome than does
individual decision making. Panels and boards of many kinds assemble
to draw on various perspectives of diverse members in order to achieve
a better informed and perhaps more responsible or balanced decision.
However, according to social-psychological research from as early as
1960, this is not always the case. In fact, it is systematically not true.

Consider Tom's board of directors contemplating a strategic acquisition. Each member has read the materials describing the strategic benefits
as well as the risks associated with the acquisition. The acquisition has
various levels of commitment that have different levels of risk associated
with them.

Because they are all busy and geographically dispersed, the directors
have had no time to consult with each other prior to the board meeting.
Each director, therefore, has formed an opinion on the matter in relative
isolation, using the materials, their knowledge of the company, whatever
experience they have with prior acquisitions, and any inclinations they may
have regarding risk. When they come together to learn more about the
proposal and begin to discuss it, we may assume that their pooled ideas
and information will lead them to an answer that is balanced, given the
probability that people will have somewhat divergent opinions and that
there will be some distribution in the amount of risk directors will think
is wise for the company to take on. Perhaps an outcome will reflect a
compromise between those who are most aggressive and those who are
most cautious in their decisions. This is what Tom expects, too.

We assume that the overall outcome for the group will resemble an
aggregation of or compromise among the individual positions the directors hold, allowing perhaps for the fact that some directors have more
influence than others and thus may swing the decision in their direction. What is not typically included in our image of this decision-making

group is that the initial positions people bring to the table, depending on which way they are leaning, have already predisposed the group decision to move further in that direction or, in other words, to become more extreme. If the individual decisions that directors have made cluster slightly on the risky side, for example, the final group decision is likely to be even riskier. If the average of the individual decisions is on the cautious side, the final group decision is likely to be even more cautious.

The Phenomenon of Group Polarization

This effect is what social psychologists call *group polarization*. It is the tendency for groups to reach collective decisions that are more extreme than the decisions the individual group members would choose to make individually. Discussion, or collectively sharing in a decision process, has the effect of moving decisions to more extreme points, in other words, producing polarization.

This phenomenon was, for many years, known as the "risky shift" phenomenon because it was initially believed to be a tendency for groups always to shift in the direction of greater risk when they engaged in group decision making.[1] It was identified in experiments in which groups had to make decisions regarding various "choice points," each of which had certain odds of success or failure (i.e., risk). Individuals were asked to choose a degree of riskiness on each choice point, and the average around which these decisions clustered was noted. The individuals then engaged in a group discussion about the problem and came to a collective decision. Risky shift referred to the fact that these collective decisions were almost always riskier than the previously noted average of the individuals' private judgments.[2] In other words, as a collective, the group had shifted its decision in the direction of taking greater risk. In addition, when individuals were asked after this discussion to articulate their own individual decision again, the average of these had also shifted to greater risk. Figure 4.1 illustrates the phenomenon.

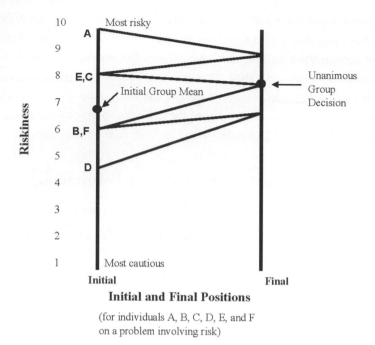

Figure 4.1. *Initial and final positions for individuals considering a problem involving risk.*

From "Risky Shift" to "Group Polarization"

Although it was believed for some time that groups without exception always shifted toward greater risk, it was soon determined that some choices led groups to shift systematically toward more cautious decisions (the "cautious shift" phenomenon). Researchers were forced to reexamine their assumptions, and it became clear that the determining factor was the actual choice dilemma—some problems seemed to have a natural bent toward risk, while others drew out an inclination toward caution. Whatever the direction, though, the effect of shifting to a more extreme position remained true. Still later, researchers realized that this shifting applied even more generally not only to problems not involving risk but also to choices about attitudes and opinions.[3] For example, one study illustrated that two groups of subjects classified as "more racially prejudiced" and "less racially prejudiced" became more extreme in their respective positions following group discussion.[4] So over time the phenomenon became known as "group polarization." Whatever the issue under discussion, groups tend to polarize in the direction toward which their individual decisions are inclined, moving the group decision more extremely in that direction. Therefore, if a group average of individual decisions clustered around a position that was slightly in favor of something (say, prayer in school), the group decision would be more strongly in favor of prayer in school.

Theory and Evidence

What are the causes of group polarization? Two primary explanations currently dominate the discussion: social comparison theory and persuasive arguments theory. Some scholars privilege one theory over another, and the two "causes" have been observed independently in lab studies. But most people agree that in the real world, group polarization results from some combination of the two.

Social Comparison Theory

The social comparison theory (SCT) explanation for group polarization is rooted in one of the fundamentals of human psychology: individuals seek to create, sustain, and present to others a self-image that is positive and consistent. Our positive self-image is created in relation to and in interaction with others, and we are constantly working to adjust and preserve it as we observe our social surroundings and as we compare ourselves particularly to relevant others.[5] As we create this self-image, we tend to think of ourselves as being more favorable than the average person. On any given dimension, we perceive ourselves as distinct and different from the average in a favorable way. Perhaps we believe we are smarter than most people. We likely believe we are nicer than most, or perhaps we believe we are more risk averse than most people if we value this. Because these self-conceptions do not happen or exist in isolation from our surroundings, our perceptions of others and the way we present ourselves are a critical component to sustaining our self-image. We attempt to present ourselves in ways that we want others to perceive us and the way we want to perceive ourselves.[6]

How does SCT relate to group polarization? Let us take an example of the risky shift. Suppose an individual director must consider among a series of five options (ranging from more to less risky) and decides that option 3 is slightly risky but not too risky. In general and as a professional, he sees himself as aggressive and competitive and as someone who is not afraid of taking on some risk. In other words, his self-image is that he is slightly more risk taking than the average colleague but not overly or irresponsibly risky. In addition, he probably sees this as a strength of his, perhaps even tying it to successes he has had in the past and to the way other people view him. In his own mind, then, he settles on option 3.

When the board convenes and discusses the matter, his fellow directors must disclose their opinions, and he realizes that most have also chosen option 3 and a few have chosen the riskier option 2. One director even pushes for option 1, the most risky. The distribution of evaluations is now public, and he realizes that it puts him at the cautious end of the spectrum, which is inconsistent with the image he has of himself. He is likely, therefore, to reassess his own evaluation of the riskiness of the various options and move toward option 2. This is more consistent with his belief that he is slightly more risk taking than most others, and it is more in line with how he wants to present himself in the group.

In summary, it may not be possible, particularly on problems where there is little concrete information or where people have little experience, for individual directors to properly assess the riskiness of a particular decision before they have seen the distribution of other people's assessments. The discussion, therefore, gives people the information they need to figure out which option they should choose if they want to present themselves to the rest of the group in a way that is consistent with their self-image—perhaps as "risk taking" or as "cautious." Social comparison then leads the individual decision maker to reassess his initial position once he becomes aware of how he compares with others on some dimension, in this case, risk taking.

We can also see from this brief description why the direction of shifting would always be in the direction of the initial mean of the group. If most of the individual evaluations and decisions are on the risky side of the spectrum, yet individuals realize that they cluster there, each person will be inclined to shift further. Whatever comparative direction is part of an individual's self-image becomes exaggerated when the positions of the others become public.

Being a risk taker, although highly valued in some settings, may be among the more benign attributes that an individual tries to portray in a given group. One can imagine decisions about diversity, race, compensation, and global strategy, where the group is essentially trying to settle on either an opposition to or a favorable stance toward something that is linked to particular attitudes. It is even easier to imagine the social comparison effect on these dimensions. Here the felt pressure to move in one direction or another may be even more acute since certain attitudes may have strong implications for one's self-concept and positive self-image.

Persuasive Arguments Theory

The second theory used to explain group polarization is the persuasive arguments theory. This theory is more straightforward and relies on the *content* of arguments put forward in group discussion. It simply suggests that the preponderance and persuasiveness of arguments that come to light in discussion and that favor a particular direction will shift the group's decision in that direction.[7] It presumes that for any given choice point, there is a pool of arguments that can be made. This total pool of arguments favors either risk or caution, or some relevant direction, on the problem under consideration.[8] When a group comes together, each individual has in mind some subset of those total arguments, reflecting the total sample but not actually containing the full set of arguments. Group discussion then allows people to become familiar with the full set of arguments. As a consequence, then, of hearing the full sample that is inclined in a particular direction, individuals shift their own positions further in this direction as well.

The total pool of arguments represents what for a factual dilemma would be the "correct" answer. Choice dilemmas, like complex decisions faced by boards of directors, obviously do not have a "correct" answer, but rather are defined by the arguments that are the most preponderant and persuasive to the group.

One obvious implication of this theory is that under some strange circumstance of unusual or skewed discussion that fails to surface something close to the "total" pool of arguments, the group could arrive at a "wrong" decision. In this case they have not benefited from the total pool of arguments relevant to the decision. Although this is not often discussed in the group polarization literature, it is easy to imagine such a "strange" circumstance in the settings we are discussing here.

Group Polarization on Boards

One of the great limitations of the group polarization research is that all of it has been conducted in controlled laboratory experiments. Little is known, therefore, about how organizational context or interpersonal dynamics may factor into the process. Anyone close to boards knows they are influenced by interpersonal dynamics! Directors are typically skilled, persuasive people who are used to having and wielding influence. In addition, people often bring some kind of expertise to the group, which gives them a disproportionate amount of influence and information with regard to particular board decisions. So how can we understand group polarization or its potential impact in the context of boards?

Based on the lab research, we can offer some predictions. First, the areas most likely to come under the effect of polarization are those on which there is some implicit norm on the board and on which no director has a clear expertise or access to information that would make a "correct" decision obvious to the other directors. When individuals are aware of something being normatively valued by the group, and by "good" members of the group, they are more likely to try to position themselves, in terms of both self-image and self-presentation, in the direction of that attitude or slightly beyond that attitude in order to be above average. Sitting inside boardrooms, it is clear that there are some matters on which boards have implicit normative commitments. These may not be overtly acknowledged, but they are ingrained. For example, many boards have a certain disdain for the interferences of what they perceive to be misinformed, overly aggressive activist shareholders. At times, boards face decisions that implicitly speak to this movement, whether it be adopting a new governance guideline, responding to some criticism in the press, or even taking a new strategic direction that these shareholders believe is self-serving or irresponsible.

One board recently faced just such a decision, whether or not to adopt a governance guideline that was considered to be "best practice." It seemed unnecessary in any practical sense for this particular board, but it also would not be detrimental or difficult to adopt. During the discussion the chairman asked all directors to express their viewpoints. Initially some board members were mildly opposed to the guideline, but over the course of discussing their opinions, the board became further and further convinced and resistant to the idea of caving to the unwarranted and unpopular pressure of the governance movement outside the boardroom. Directors began to position their arguments more and more in terms of the attitude of defiance and frustration the board felt toward needing to meet requirements simply to symbolically follow governance expectations. Only the chairman's intervention, at the end of the discussion, refocused the directors on their goals as a board to be at the forefront of good governance and on the notion that this guideline was in accordance with those goals. Implicitly, it appeared the board supported an attitude of disdain for the rhetoric of governance gurus, and as a group they shifted further and further toward this norm, almost undermining their ultimate intent as a board. Topics like this, where a particular board has adopted a normative stance, or where it is clear what attitude is valued and respected in the boardroom, are the ones most likely to be subject to polarization.

A second matter that may be of consequence for boards is the aspect of how directors relate to one another. Some scholars have argued that social comparison only leads people to move to a more extreme position in their decision if they believe they are similar to others in the group in attributes relevant to the judgment being made. For example, if it is assumed that risk taking is linked with talent, creativity, and ability, then individuals would polarize to risk more if they believed others in the group were similar to them on these attributes.[9] Most boards are quite homogeneous and are likely to perceive themselves as similar on these kinds of relevant attributes and background experiences. In other words, those that are most socially cohesive are also most subject to possible polarization effects.

Preventing Group Polarization from Undermining Board Decision Making

Polarization is not desirable from a decision-making perspective simply because it results in decisions that do not accurately reflect the desires, opinions, or attitudes of the individuals who make up the group. From a governance perspective, and given the goals of assembling a board of directors, this is a clear detriment. There are a few things boards can do to minimize the likelihood that polarization will occur:

1. Ensure that there is a diversity of expertise in the boardroom. Having diversity, not only in industry experience and professional background, but also in functional, cultural, and geographic areas, increases the likelihood that, for a given problem, there is a board member who can provide meaningful information (e.g., facts, statistics, experience) on which other directors may base their own decisions. Group polarization is most likely to occur when there is little information or knowledge about a particular predicament. When a problem is novel, people are more likely to rely on each other for cues about where the norm is.

2. Eliminate the self-presentation aspect of group decision making. This means either taking a blind vote or simply having each board member report his or her position to the chairperson and reaching some outcome in this way. This is likely to be an unpalatable solution for many boards, but considering alternative ways to share information so that the source is not identifiable may minimize the social comparison effects that drive polarization.

3. Consider having board members articulate their individual positions on important items to a chairperson prior to discussion so that their positions will have been noted. This way a chairperson can be more critical of the group decision process.

It is important to note that group polarization is not a phenomenon of conformity or even of persuasiveness on the part of some group member or leader. For this reason it may be even more subtle and dangerous than the other "blind spots" discussed in this book. It is a group tendency that should be kept in mind by the board chairperson and by individual directors as they reach collective conclusions about items ranging from important strategic decisions to internal board matters.

CHAPTER 5

Groupthink

As board member Harvey Jackson prepared for the upcoming meeting of the board of Altonerics Inc., he was a little uneasy. One of the topics on the agenda for this meeting was a proposed option exchange program, originally designed by the company's head of human resources, Martha Radcliffe, at the request of the Altonerics's CEO. The program offered all Altonerics employees and directors the option of exchanging their underwater options for an equal number of shares of new options with a strike price equal to the closing price on Altonerics stock on June 2. The new options would have a vesting schedule that added 12 months to the original vesting schedule. The total number of options that would be exchanged in this program was expected to be slightly less than 5% of the total number of Altonerics's shares currently outstanding.

Harvey understood why company executives had proposed the program—primarily to address apparently growing employee morale problems caused in part by the precipitous drop in Altonerics's stock price, almost 90% in the past year. But he was uneasy because he didn't think that shareholders, if they were asked, would be in favor of this program.

Martha had presented the proposal to the board at the last meeting, and she had mentioned that Altonerics could face some negative press regarding the exchange. Similar programs at other companies had been criticized, and boards had come under fire for "expensive giveaways to management and directors at a time when shareholders had suffered." Harvey was aware of this criticism as well and had raised it briefly at the prior meeting, even before Martha's presentation.

The CEO and other six directors scoffed at the notion they were not considering shareholder interests. They argued that media and shareholder activists did not understand the issues and were constantly attacking boards because they were easy targets. Why should they take into account these image issues when they were taking their governance role seriously? They were a group of accomplished directors, and they had played an important part in moving Altonerics forward, even if there were some competitive and environmental pressures affecting performance right now. One director spoke for most of the group when he said, "Harvey, you can't listen to that stuff. We know more about what is best for this company than outsiders like analysts and institutional shareholders."

As the time for a final discussion and vote approached, a few directors jabbed Harvey, asking if he was wearing his director hat today or whether he was going to be the public relations advocate. Harvey chuckled. They were probably right. Not all decisions had clear answers, and certainly this group of directors had been nothing but good for the company.

In the board meeting, Martha again explained the reasons for the option exchange program. The directors nodded in agreement. The CEO again voiced support for the program, and several minutes later the option exchange program was unanimously approved.

The Groupthink Phenomenon

The decision outcome in the previously described example is not necessarily a bad one, although most corporate governance rating services, such as RiskMetrics, and many shareholder activists almost always oppose stock option exchange programs like this, particularly with such lucrative terms (e.g., exchange for equal numbers of shares, top executives and directors eligible for exchange). But what should be clear is that the decision process was flawed. The alternatives were not presented to and considered by the board members, and there was little discussion of the specific option presented. The proposal was seemingly summarily approved.

While several explanations could be applied to this decision-process example, one possibility is *groupthink*. The example does not describe a major disaster like some of those commonly blamed on groupthink, such as the Bay of Pigs fiasco or the Japanese high command's decision to bomb Pearl Harbor in World War II.[1] But flawed decision processes such as that described in the previous example, with outcomes that objective outsiders might not agree with, are common in corporate boardrooms. Some of them are caused by groupthink.

Groupthink is a decision-making pathology. It can be defined as "a mode of thinking [where pressure for unanimity] overwhelms the members' motivation to realistically appraise alternative courses of action."[2] Because discussions sometimes lead to polarization rather than moderation in views, groupthink can be seen as related to, and even as a specific example of, the larger class of problems called "group polarization," discussed in chapter 4. But by itself, groupthink is arguably the single most widely publicized application of psychological principles to group decision making.

At a basic level, groupthink is caused by social pressure and an inherent tendency for most people to want to avoid confrontation. As one director explained, "It's hard to sit in a room and disagree with people you respect who think it's okay."[3]

Some people cite Asch's early (1951) experimental studies on social pressure, described in chapter 3, as the earliest studies of groupthink.[4] The Asch studies demonstrated that individuals often conform to majority viewpoints, not only because they do not trust their own perceptions, but also because they do not want to stand out from the crowd for fear of being ridiculed. However, most experts use the term groupthink to indicate much more than just this simple kind of social pressure and conformity. Even where boards comprise solely individuals who are resistant to peer pressure, as some of Asch's student subjects were, groupthink would still be a concern. The modern characterization of groupthink involves a tightly knit group that is isolated from outside influences and that suffers from and acts on shared illusions. The group members, who are confident of their group's wisdom and decision-making capabilities, and hence the general invulnerability of its conclusions, converge rapidly to a normatively "correct" point of view. They fail to seek and discuss alternatives. They tend not to seek outside advice because they are convinced of the inferiority of all competing opinions (and groups). Sometimes they even engage in negative stereotyping of the outside groups. So among the key characteristics of groupthink are selective group attention, opinion polarization, the seeking of concurrence, and the suppression of dissent.[5]

The dynamics of groupthink processes are complex. Almost inevitably there must be pressures brought on dissenters to conform to the consensus view. These pressures will create individual self-censorship in the interest of "getting along" with the group and selective group attention. The pressure to conform might even invoke the pluralistic ignorance bias that was discussed in an earlier chapter as, to avoid the sanctions accorded dissenters, individuals might publicly endorse decisions and attitudes that they view as being held by the group. Whatever the reason, in a groupthink situation, dissenters remain silent, and silence is interpreted as agreement. This creates an illusion of unanimity, which, in turn, leads the group to the conclusion that their view is the only valid one. This, in turn, creates a sense of invulnerability and excessive optimism that encourages risk taking and tends to stifle creative search for other opinions. If other opinions arise, there is a tendency for the group members to reject the contrary opinions overtly and to ridicule their sources, both internal and external.

Groupthink can infect healthy decision-making groups and render them ineffective. The results of groupthink can be disastrous because it leads to carelessness and poor decisions. Relevant information, alternatives, consequences, risks, or all of these are not fully considered. The outcome is irrational thinking and action.

The Causes of Groupthink

Unanimity regarding the exact set of conditions that causes groupthink, or that causes its effects to be more severe, does not yet exist. The early academic leader on the groupthink topic, Irving Janis, suggested that four basic characteristics create an environment that increases the probability, intensity, or both of a dysfunctional groupthink decision process. First, the decision-making group is very *cohesive*. Cohesion is enhanced by homogeneity in the group members' social background, experiences, and ideology. Cohesion limits the group's diversity of views. It also creates a culture of cordiality where questioning the assumptions or conclusions of another group member is seen as impolite and inappropriate. Groups that lack cohesion can make poor decisions too, but they do not experience groupthink.

Second, the group is *insulated from outside sources of information* and analysis. This insulation promotes the development of perspectives and solutions that are possibly unique and flawed. It also causes the group to frame alternative external views as ridiculous and inadequate as there is no engagement with outside information.

Third, the group's *leader is strong and directive*. Whether overtly biased toward a specific outcome or not, she or he sets the agenda and limits the discussion to preconceived opinions so as to shape the outcome of the process rather than ensuring that everyone in the group is able to have their say.

And finally, the group is under *stress*, which might be caused by a crisis, external threats, recent failures, a need to make a decision quickly, or all of these factors. The stress causes tension and anxiety, which, in turn, causes the group members to react in less than logical ways, such as by minimizing negative information and rationalizing their choices.

To illustrate the importance of the phenomenon, Janis claimed that groupthink was responsible for the faulty decisions that led to some of the biggest tragedies in the history of the United States. His groupthink examples were all major political disasters, including the attempted invasion of the Bay of Pigs in 1961, the escalation of the Vietnam War in 1965, the Watergate break-in and cover-up in 1973, and the explosion of the *Challenger* space shuttle in 1986. In the *Challenger* space shuttle case, for example, NASA engineers knew about the dangers of conducting a launch in 36-degree weather but chose to minimize them because of pressures from NASA's top executives not to delay further the historic mission. Later writers have added other political examples. For example, Baron cited the Bush administration's decision to invade Iraq as a similar failure.[6] The White House decision-making group thought that the invasion and rebuilding of Iraq would be relatively easy and rapid, that Iraqi oil would offset many of the costs of the rebuilding, and that the Iraqi people would be thankful and cooperative. The reality, of course, has been far different. In all of these cases, cohesion and homogeneity in these cabinet- or high-level decision-making groups was very high, the leadership was not impartial, and group norms favoring methodical search processes did not exist. These conditions created tendencies for groupthink-like concurrence.

There is less than complete agreement that all the antecedent elements of Janis's model—group cohesion, insulation, directive leadership, decision-making stress—are necessary for groupthink to exist. Janis built his groupthink model based almost exclusively on historical material and, particularly, eyewitness accounts by participants. This research method has its limitations because participants' reports are incomplete and possibly biased, and reliance solely on archival evidence can lead to a hindsight bias. Other researchers have attempted to test Janis's model, but because of its complexity, few tests of the entire model have been conducted.

Considerable research has, however, focused on the individual elements of the model. This research has found that each of Janis's antecedent conditions *can* lead to groupthink behavior, but they do not necessarily do so. For example, even when considering multiple forms of cohesiveness, such as group identification, social attraction, and personal friendship, researchers have not always found high cohesion to be dysfunctional.[7] Similarly, while crisis conditions do increase the likelihood that directive leaders will be more prone to offer their own solutions and push for a rapid decision rather than free discussion, crises do not ensure that groupthink will occur. Moreover, the severity of crisis does not necessarily correlate with decision quality.

Almost everyone believes that the groupthink phenomenon exists and that it can have powerful effects. The groupthink symptoms seem to resonate with most people's own personal experiences. Many and perhaps even most groups suffer from some of the symptoms of groupthink, such as the polarization of positions, the suppression of discussion and dissent, and poor decision quality.

A number of researchers have suggested modifications to Janis's groupthink model. One of the first and most credible revisions of Janis's ideas came from Glen Whyte. Whyte argued that the most important antecedent is not group cohesiveness, as in Janis's model, but rather *perceived collective efficacy*. Perceived collective efficacy reflects the strength of a group's belief in its capability to perform a given task successfully. The most important factor affecting perceptions of collective efficacy is past performance. Perceptions of collective efficacy spiral upward based

on perceived past successes. Repeated successes, particularly in like decision situations, give groups confidence in their abilities. Perceptions of
collective efficacy are also affected by individuals' perceptions of their
own abilities and those of their fellow group members and, particularly,
the group leader.

Very highly perceived collective efficacy, which can be interpreted as
feelings of overconfidence or even invulnerability, tends to create problems. It can lead to complacency, decreased search and attention, and
hence, groupthink. Whyte reinterpreted some of the same examples
cited by Janis, including the Cuban missile crisis, the Watergate cover-up,
and the space shuttle *Challenger* disaster, and pointed out that highly perceived collective efficacy was present in each of these situations.

One of the most recent groupthink-related contributions comes from
Robert Baron.[8] Baron suggested that groupthink is more pervasive and
important than even Janis envisioned. He argued that the reason people continue to discuss the groupthink phenomenon even in the face of
conflicting empirical evidence regarding the importance of some of the
individual elements of his model is because groupthink is nearly "ubiquitous." Janis's antecedent conditions occur commonly in most "everyday"
group decision-making situations, although not necessarily all controlled
laboratory situations. If so, then groupthink should be considered as a
widespread and critically important problem faced by nearly all "real
world" decision-making groups.

Baron recast Janis's model into one with three conditions that are
deemed to be necessary and sufficient to create groupthink.[9] The first factor is *social identification*. Individuals have social identification when they
feel part of the group. The social identification, in turn, provokes feelings
of allegiance and increased pressures for conformity.

The second necessary condition is the presence of *salient norms*, phil-
osophical or attitudinal homogeneity. Baron claims that after the 9/11
attacks on the World Trade Center, the members of President George
W. Bush's administration developed a shared philosophy regarding the
wisdom of using preemptive military interventions. This led to the inva-
sions of both Iraq and Afghanistan despite the strong objections of many
Americans and American allies. Baron considers these decisions to be
groupthink failures.

The third necessary condition is *low situational self-efficacy*, which is where "group members generally lack confidence in their ability to reach satisfactory resolution of the conundrum facing them."[10] When situational self-efficacy is low, the effects of social influence tend to be greater. Individuals are less likely to take a risk by speaking out unless they feel extremely confident about their own positions. The lack of confidence provides them with even more reason to suppress their dissent using the argument "all those folks can't be wrong."[11]

Baron deemed Janis's other antecedent factors—crisis, intense cohesion, insulation, directive leadership, and crisis—not to be necessary for a groupthink condition, although they might increase the likelihood or intensity of groupthink. Baron's work suggests that there are multiple paths to the creation of groupthink.

At this point, none of these groupthink models has been tested in its entirety. But while there are differences among the models, in some sense they reinforce each other. The key points are that the groupthink phenomenon exists, it is an important decision-making pathology, and a small number of factors descriptive of the group and its decision setting affect both the likelihood of facing groupthink and the severity of the problem where it is faced.

Groupthink in the Boardroom

Is groupthink common in the decision-making processes of corporate boards? Boardrooms are notoriously difficult for researchers to penetrate, so detailed analyses of decision-making processes like those done on political decisions are rare. But the answer to this question is almost assuredly yes: Boardrooms seem to create conditions in which groupthink is likely, if not nearly inevitable in some decision situations.

Enron, for example, provided fertile ground for groupthink to take hold, and perhaps the causes of groupthink in the Enron board were different in the earlier and later years of that company's history. Unquestionably, Enron's aggressive and competitive culture led to a strong appetite for earnings, and by all objective measures, including growth in revenues, profits, and market capitalization, the company was very successful for a long period of time. Investors cheered. The media held Enron and its managers out as paragons of excellence. Enron was "consistently voted the most innovative large company in America in *Fortune*'s Most Admired Companies survey."[12] Regulators looked the other way. The successes gave the management team the illusion of invulnerability, and the board members probably attributed some of that success to the company's excellent system of governance. Indeed, Enron's system of governance had some nice traits. The board comprised many highly competent individuals, the company's financial reports were audited by a prestigious Big-5 auditing firm, and the company had a well-regarded code of ethics.

In this sense, the more recent failure of Satyam Computer Systems is eerily similar to that of Enron. Satyam had been highly successful, and the company was seen to have a prestigious, blue-chip board. Shortly before its failure, Satyam was awarded the Golden Peacock Award for Excellence in Corporate Governance by the Institute of Directors.[13] High perceptions of collective efficacy probably discouraged board members from asking the right questions.

Just before Enron's failure, a different set of causes of groupthink, as reflected in the Baron groupthink model, seemed to have arisen. Enron management had created "new paradigms," "killer apps," and a plethora of esoteric financial instruments that few people understood. The arrogant personalities of Enron's top managers such as CEO Jeffrey Skilling discouraged anyone from questioning the company's innovative management practices. Most of the few who did either resigned or were fired. These factors probably lowered the board's perceived collective self-efficacy and increased the·individual board members' willingness to go along with the judgments of the group.

In the size of the problems created, the Enron and Satyam examples are outliers. But in other ways perhaps they are not so much outliers. Boardroom settings are in some important ways quite similar to one another. Most have the antecedent conditions that are necessary and sufficient to create groupthink according to one or more of the groupthink researchers. Board members almost invariably have common social identifications. Many of them come from their similar social backgrounds, their identification as professional board members, and their identification with the group with which they are serving. Boards also have salient norms. Most board members believe in genteel, consensus-based decision-making practices. They typically express unqualified support for the CEO.[14] Open dissent is rare in a boardroom. Other norms are derived from the philosophies of the board members' own corporations, such as the emphasis placed on customer service, product quality, aggressive pricing, or the value placed on diversity.

And collective self-efficacy can swing dramatically from one extreme to another depending on the issue at hand. In normal times, collective self-efficacy is quite high. Boards comprise highly competent individuals who naturally believe in their own abilities and those of their fellow board members, and periods of success increase those feelings of efficacy. But when problems occur and intensify, perceptions of collective self-efficacy can become very low. Even the best board members often find themselves at an information or knowledge disadvantage that should force them to seek input from, for example, technology, industry, accounting, or legal experts. In such cases, board members fear sanctions when challenging either the expert in the room or group norms. They are unlikely to speak up unless they feel extremely confident about their opinions. But in such cases of high ambiguity and complexity, they probably do not have that confidence.

Ways to Minimize Groupthink in Boardrooms

Theories suggest ways to prevent groupthink in the boardroom or, at least, to minimize its effects. It can be done by eliminating or weakening the so-called antecedent conditions, which are summarized in Table 5.1.

This understanding suggests that the potential for groupthink can be minimized by taking any or all the following steps, which are differentiable but not necessarily unrelated:

1. Include on the board people who have different backgrounds and who are likely to have different viewpoints. This can weaken group cohesion (Janis's term) and social identity and salient norms (Baron's terms). The idea of mandating a minimum number of professional directors, taken from a list approved by a government regulatory committee, on boards and various board committees arises periodically, particularly soon after a wave of financial scandals. Using professional directors can also reduce the potential to form particularly destructive, highly cohesive "inner circles" of board members.[15]

Table 5.1. Antecedents of Groupthink According to the Models of Janis (1982) and Baron (2005)

Janis	Baron
Cohesive decision-making group	Social identification
Insulation from outside sources of information and analysis	Salient norms
Directive group leader	Low situational self-efficacy
Decision-making stress	

2. Ensure that the information on which boards base decisions comes from sources other than the CEO, and advisors or consultants who are CEO loyalists can reduce the insulation from outside sources of information and analysis (Janis's term).

3. Design a decision process to ensure that a range of alternatives are considered can reduce insulation (Janis's term) and break down some dysfunctional social norms (Baron's term). In some cases, particularly critical decisions where confidentiality either is unnecessary or can be preserved, it is desirable to allow outside experts to contribute. In some cases, board members might be encouraged to discuss the issue with trusted people outside the board. In other cases, the board should invite outside experts into the board meetings.

4. Create and maintain a boardroom culture in which the board members are both empowered and have the expectation that they will debate and challenge each other can overcome the deleterious effects of group cohesion (Janis's term). It is not enough to have board member diversity; that diversity in skills, perceptions, and ideas must be used. To the extent possible, board members must feel free to speak out without fear of being ostracized. In some critical cases, a single issue can be assigned to several board subgroups for consideration and possibly presentation.

Some of this culture will stem from the board leadership. Either the chair or the lead independent director should adopt a neutral role, which includes not expressing an opinion when opening a discussion or assigning a task. The leader should encourage the expression of minority viewpoints. The leader can go further and assign the role of "critical evaluator" or "devil's advocate" to one board member, or possibly even to every board member. Formally assigning this role to someone will prevent the isolation that would be felt by someone who voluntarily assumed this role. Alternatively, the board can hire outside, independent experts to play this contrary role, to provide a critical appraisal of the group's choices. These evaluators provide a "reality check" that guards against the possibility of groupthink.

5. Include important knowledge experts on the board to enhance the boards' collective self-efficacy (Baron's term). Education and training can be done at both the individual and the board level. Self-efficacy can also be improved by including on the board experts on the issues being faced. If research and development is important, then technical expertise should be included on the board. If selling to a particular industry is important, then two or more board members with experience in that industry can be recruited. If accounting problems are critical, then the board should probably include multiple "financial experts."

The groupthink phenomenon is definitely one that board leaders, members, and consultants should understand and prepare to deal with. But like many of the pathologies described in this book, groupthink is a difficult force to deal with. The factors that cause it are often functional. For example, some degree of social cohesion and conformity keeps boards from endless bickering and power struggles. But too much cohesion is a common cause of groupthink. The challenge is to strike a healthy balance and to use other mechanisms to guard against the groupthink problems.

CHAPTER 6

Group Habitual Routines

As Andrew left his hotel room and headed to the elevator, he mulled over the issues that would likely come up at the board dinner tonight. He had already decided how he felt about the acquisition proposed by CEO Todd Harvey, but he wondered whether his fellow directors were similarly negative about it. He was eager to get past the "wine-and-dine schmooze event" starting at 7 o'clock at the hotel bistro. It would probably be a late night, but at least he knew what to expect. After Harvey and the senior managers of Arksey & Co. left the restaurant, Andrew and the other directors would retire to the bar, have a few drinks, and sooner or later the dirt would start to fly.

Although he was tired, as lead independent director, he knew he could not miss what was essentially the "real board meeting." Every quarter, when the outside board members gathered at the bar after dinner, they discussed with candor their concerns and ideas. It was not unusual—in fact, it was quite routine—to move through the entire board meeting the following day without hearing any of the "real" concerns directors had. CEO Harvey had a powerful personality. He was not the easiest person to criticize, and all in all, the board did not like experiencing tension with him in these board meetings. Andrew and the others relied on the premeeting "meetings" at the bar to assure themselves that they were fulfilling their director roles and to voice their contributions on the issues facing Arksey. Typically the actual content of these meetings would get back to Harvey through informal channels and in a watered-down version less likely to ruffle his feathers.

The Concept of Routine Behavior

Most of us intuitively recognize and understand the concept of routine behavior. Humans are creatures of habit. We have experienced the process of performing a task, perhaps brushing our teeth, pulling the car out of the garage, or even driving to work, in a habitual, relatively "mindless" manner. We may have completed the task before we are even aware of having started it and perform the various parts of the task with very little cognitive effort or attention. Routinizing behavior has some advantages. It is an important way of organizing action, and it can save time and energy. However, it can also lead to mindless behavior and inflexibility or inability to respond to extraordinary or unusual circumstances.

The concept of routine behavior extends beyond individuals to various kinds of collectivities including organizations and also groups, which, of course, is the subject here. Groups, just like individuals, are susceptible to developing habitual routines, whereby particular tasks are performed with unchanging routine behavior and a relatively disengaged state of mind. From a group perspective, we consider a habitual routine to exist when "a group repeatedly exhibits a functionally similar pattern of behavior in a given stimulus situation without explicitly selecting it over alternative ways of behaving."[1] Academic work on habitual routines in groups has been limited, but theoretical papers and our own observations provide the groundwork for this chapter. Some of what is known about individual habitual behaviors can also be extrapolated to the group level.

A vivid example of a group habitual routine comes from Gersick and Hackman.[2] Their story is that of Air Florida Flight 90, which, shortly after taking off from Washington National Airport in January 1982, crashed into a bridge over the Potomac River. All 74 passengers and crewmembers died. The official cause of the accident as cited by the National Transportation Safety Board was (a) that the crew failed to use the engine anti-ice process prior to and during takeoff and (b) that the captain did not abort the takeoff despite "anomalous engine instrument readings." The flight had been delayed almost 2 hours because of a snowstorm that caused the airport to shut down temporarily.

Analyses of cockpit voice recordings showed that the first officer and the captain engaged with the typical pretakeoff checklist, the first officer stating prompts and the captain responding as he checked various indicators. Proceeding routinely through the checklist, when prompted with the "anti-ice" item, the captain responded "off." What is notable, of course, is that the routine response for the anti-ice prompt, something pilots and first officers check every time they take off—multiple times a day and hundreds of times a year—is "off," particularly for those flying in warm climates. Despite discussing only minutes later how cold the weather was and that they might need wipers, the first officer and captain were operating so routinely in their pretakeoff ritual that they failed actively to recode the situation in which they were flying.

Another aspect of routine behavior was revealed in the minutes following, when the first officer, who was actually piloting the aircraft in this case, called attention to an instrument reading that was not normal. The captain first ignored the first officer's concern then dismissed a second attempt. The first officer ended the exchange still not convinced, saying, "Naw, I don't think that's right," but he continued with the takeoff anyway. This interaction suggests that the takeoff routine was so resilient that two experienced pilots were able to ignore evidence that breaking the routine and aborting the takeoff may have been the appropriate action. It also illustrates how difficult it may be to raise the idea of interrupting a routine. The first officer's concerns hardly registered with the captain.

To be sure, habitual routines can be functional in groups, but at the same time, they can facilitate undesired consequences like the plane crash just described. What is important from our perspective is (a) to understand that habitual routines are a frequent and important part of group behavior and (b) to anticipate conditions under which routines may emerge or may need to change so that boards can avoid crisis and also perform up to their capabilities.

Certainly boards have many easily recognized routines: meetings at the exact same time of year, a dinner the night before the meeting, a board book sent to directors prior to the meeting, some introduction to management at the site of the meeting, committee sessions prior to the full board meeting, coffee breaks where directors engage in brief dialogue about their professional lives, and so on. Many board members sit in the same seat at every meeting. Some board members are expected to say little. Some of these routines are functional. Others exist partly because of habit and partly because those involved have busy calendars, making changes difficult.

Some routines exist visibly, explicitly, and for obvious reasons. However, there are also more subtle routines that become a part of a board's process. Moreover, those routines that are indeed visible sometimes fulfill a function that is not immediately obvious.

Academics like to distinguish between those aspects of group process that are oriented toward the *task* of the group and those that are aimed toward the *social* or *socioemotional* needs of the group.[3] In other words, boards may have routines that emerge around the tasks they do—perhaps a particular routine for delivering and discussing committee reports or for approving CEO compensation—as well as routines oriented toward the preservation and social needs of the group. A socially oriented routine may be using humor to defuse conflict, for example. Perhaps when a particular board gets into an uncomfortable moment of tension and conflict, a director cracks a joke and the board can reestablish comfort among the group members and move past the conflict, with or without resolving it. This is an example of a board acting toward its socioemotional needs, to maintain the order and comfort of the group.

Task-oriented routines, not surprisingly, are often more visible than socially motivated routines. However, both task- and socially oriented routines can be challenging to change or even to identify, particularly by a member of the group in question. The vignette at the beginning of this chapter illustrates a routine that likely serves both task and socioemotional needs. It helps the board along both lines, but it can also lead it into trouble. Perhaps directors are mildly aware of what they are doing, taking meaningful and potentially conflicting discussion out of the full board meeting.

Perhaps some of them recognize that the reason they do this is because of their rather tense relationship with the CEO and the lack of strong, independent leadership on the board. It is easily imaginable that this board—either because it assumes it has an effective process (a routine) for getting directors to voice concerns or because their routine actively suppresses in-meeting, real-time voicing of dissent in the presence of the CEO—could be underperforming and also could fail in a way that leads into crisis.

The complex and relatively invisible nature of habitual routines make them an extremely important topic for boards. Next we explore the causes, benefits, and perils of group habitual routines and how we may experience and act on them in the context of boards.

Understanding the Phenomenon

Sociologists and psychologists explain the development and persistence of habitual behavior in a variety of ways. They are not necessarily exclusive of one another; however, each offers us a different perspective on why routines may be not only important but also problematic for group behavior and for boards more specifically.

Efficiency

If we take a functional perspective, habitual routines emerge because they are functionally important to the group or to an organization. For example, routines are considered to make action more efficient because they reduce the amount of energy people must spend cognitively searching for information or considering what actions should be taken. Routines reduce complexity for individuals and groups so action may be taken more quickly and with less effort. People cannot continually process all the complexity that underlies social behavior and therefore develop heuristics, short cuts, and other conscious and unconscious ways of reducing this complexity. The fact that individuals must manage their "bounded rationality" using cognitive tools is one of the fundamental truths of human behavior and of organizational theory.[4]

Habitual routines fall into this category of reducing complexity. Routines are sometimes referred to as "scripts" because they tell us how to behave in certain situations. For example, we may see a woman running down the sidewalk in high heels and with a ripped blouse, and we instantly code the situation as an "emergency." There are certain cues that lead us to code it this way without active cognitive effort. The cues activate a script for how to behave. For example, in this situation we might approach her to offer help or call 911. If the same woman were to run past us in running shoes and a T-shirt, we might barely notice her because our unconscious coding of the situation does not prime us to act. March and Simon famously termed this understanding of human behavior "the logic of appropriateness." Individuals code situations and their role in the situation and act according to what is appropriate for someone like them to do in that situation.

Legitimacy

Another reason routines emerge is because they lend legitimacy to a particular group or organization as an institution.[5] This idea is rooted in institutional theory, which posits that organizations come to resemble each other because they mimic structures and processes of successful organizations. These structures and processes become institutionalized over time, taken for granted as the way things are done, and organizations that adopt them gain legitimacy through doing so. For example, the development of the various C-positions (CEO, CFO, CIO) that now exist in virtually every company can be seen in such a light.

For boards of directors, prior to legislation that made it a requirement, the adoption of board evaluation processes might be such an example. As highly visible and seemingly effective boards with high-status directors began to list board evaluation as part of their governance objectives, more and more boards began to adopt similar guidelines for director evaluation. Shareholder activists undoubtedly were a part of this shift, in large part by publishing what "effective" boards were doing and shaming others into following suit. Under institutional theory, the more pressure and the more uncertainty that surrounds an entity, the more likely it is to mimic others like it that are perceived to be successful. One of the "dysfunctions" inherent in this legitimacy model is that practices are adopted to achieve external legitimacy, while the actual internal organizational behavior remains unchanged. Those familiar with boards in the 1990s and early 2000s might attest to precisely this phenomenon: where board evaluation processes were formally adopted but were basically meaningless activities.

Reducing Conflict

A third reason routines may emerge and be sustained over time is because they avoid the renegotiation of power dynamics every time a particular task must be performed. Nelson and Winter have termed this "routines as truce."[6] Once the division of roles, sequences of tasks, and areas of influence and authority have been determined, they will remain that way going forward, allowing the group to reduce the amount of conflict it must deal with at every turn. Individuals or departments will not feel as threatened in their authority or be as inclined to negotiate when a routine has been established for a long time. Of course, this does not mean that lines will not be redrawn at some stage, but routines may be a way in which organizations reduce conflict.

Ease of Use and Success

A fourth reason deserves mention here as well. Not only does it come from the organizational literature, but it also has a parallel line of argument in psychology. This reason is that a particular context simply makes a certain way of doing something easier than another. This becomes the process of choice and is repeated.[7] Over time it may become supported by formal structures and other processes, which then make it even more resistant to change.

An important outgrowth of this point is that behaviors and routines repeat themselves to the extent that they are successful. Psychologists have explored the question of how routines are maintained both in individual settings and in groups and organizations. Psychologist Ellen Langer's work, for example, notes that when the environment or the problem to be dealt with remains relatively unchanged, repeated success with a particular action leads to routine behavior.[8] In fact, simply not receiving negative feedback can be enough to produce a routine.[9] Over time, through repetition and perceived success, people develop confidence in the validity and effectiveness of their response, so they repeat it.

Langer's work focuses specifically on cognitive engagement. Simply stated, when there is little uncertainty in the environment, there is little new information to process and cognitive activity is lower.[10] As a result, people fall into what she calls "mindless" behavior, repeating actions coded onto a certain situation without actively recoding the situation or reevaluating the appropriateness of the behaviors.

How Habitual Routines Affect Boards

Routines obviously can provide benefits for groups. In fact, routinized behavior is essential to group and organizational functioning because individuals must be able to predict to some degree how their colleagues will act in order to coordinate behavior.[11] Boards can save a great deal of time and energy by breezing through certain aspects of their collective work with well-rehearsed and repetitive behaviors. Many approvals that come to the board are routine; others are too detailed and complex to warrant detailed attention by busy directors. Knowingly or unknowingly adopting a routine set of questions and testing mechanisms for management may free the board to take on more important matters and to "keep their eye on the ball," so to speak.

However, as we have seen previously, there are potential pitfalls, and boards are certainly susceptible to them. First, a habitual routine can prevent boards from adjusting when conditions change and require different behaviors or processes. In other words, boards may perform the same behaviors and ask the same questions, even though they are no longer appropriate to the situation. The story of Flight 90 presents just such an example, and potentially so does the board vignette at the beginning of this chapter.

When Routines Emerge on Boards

One necessary condition for the emergence of a routine is constant and frequent repetition of a particular function. A reasonable question might be whether boards meet often enough and do enough repetitive tasks to develop habitual routines in the first place. We believe they do. The tasks are not as minute and identifiable as checking the "anti-ice" setting, but they are recognizable, highly salient because of their importance, and easily coded by board members.

The activities on boards that are most vulnerable to developing routines are those that occur frequently and with regularity and those at which the board perceives itself to be successful, or at least receives no direct negative feedback. Unfortunately, boards rarely receive immediate negative feedback, so most are likely to perceive themselves to be fairly successful in the absence of major crisis or negative publicity.

In terms of regularity, several board activities suggest themselves. On the *task* front, "minor" approvals (e.g., minutes of prior meetings, small appropriation requests) and committee reports are on the agenda of every meeting. Boards likely vote on some management proposal or item of strategic importance at each board meeting and also may have to approve stock decisions regarding stock management on a somewhat regular basis. They also regularly have executive sessions where independent directors discuss concerns and questions they want to raise, but only with other directors, not (yet) with the CEO directly. These are tasks that may lend themselves to routine behavior. For one oil and mineral company we know, one of the matters that consistently came to the board was approval of new geographic investments, based on estimates and predictions of how much could be extracted from them. This was an easily identifiable process as it always appeared on the agenda under the same designator, and it required the same kinds of questions from board members who wanted to ensure it was a good and responsible investment.

At another level, there are certain *group* events that happen frequently and repetitively on boards. For example, each meeting is likely to see a difference of opinion among the directors on some matter. In addition, most meetings may have instances during which directors disagree about the process they are using. Some directors may be going for greater depth of information from management than others feel is necessary or appropriate. At some points, a director may be dwelling on an idea or discussion longer than others want to. How boards navigate these kinds of group tensions or discomforts may become routine over time, in a way that is not even noticeable to board members.

One board, for example, dealt with disagreement and tension by invoking the distinction of roles between the board and management. This was nearly always the way in which contentious issues were "resolved." The point of disagreement would remain, but one of the directors would state abstractly that "the board should govern and management should manage," and hence the discussion ended. This board had adopted a routine for dealing with disagreement and almost never departed from it, even though the kinds of issues under discussion varied widely and may have called for different kinds of "resolution." It was easy to see not only that the board was avoiding tension but also that it could have been performing at a higher level by forcing itself, at times, to address conflict head on—taking a position on important strategic assumptions and questions that would surface again. It is easy to see how this kind of routine for addressing disagreement, if applied to the wrong issue, could have led this board to crisis down the road.

Of course, this habitual routine for dealing with differences may have been very useful for the board. Digging into every source of conflict is draining; it uses up scarce energy and time, and it can be demoralizing. And, indeed, some conflicts do not need to be resolved as long as the board can move forward together. However, some areas of conflict reveal deep underlying assumptions about the success of the company, the role of the board, the competence of management, and strategic direction. It is important for the board to be able to switch gears when something that requires more than the typical response emerges. Unfortunately, this is precisely the place where the routine prevents the kind of "mindful" scanning of the environment and cognitive engagement that can make a shift in gears possible.

One example, which has been cited previously,[12] is that of the Enron board. In June 1999, the Enron directors collectively approved a proposal by CFO Andy Fastow to suspend the company's code of ethics. This approval was certainly one that warranted a different kind of deliberation, but the issue was brought up among a slew of other items "jam packed" into a 1-hour telephone board meeting. The decision turned out to be devastating to Enron and its stakeholders. The board was not in the critical frame of mind that would have led to a discussion about this *unique* request. Rather, it was coded as a routine, time-sensitive approval, of which a board sees many.

Directors, by their own accounts, are no strangers to the practice of raising important, potentially contentious matters at the very end of a board meeting. During this time the directors are distracted, eager to leave, and primed to approve routine matters that just "need to get done." This is precisely the kind of tactic that preys on routine and cognitive disengagement. However, as conveyed in this chapter, a habitual routine does not require purposive action by an eager CEO/chairperson to create problems for a board. Habitual routines emerge in the ordinary course of group interaction. They are usually invisible, and they are difficult to change. How can boards avoid the dysfunctional aspects of this inherent part of group process? This is where we turn next.

Avoiding Negative Aspects

Ideally a group should try to benefit from the efficiency and group well-being aspects of habitual routines but avoid the probability that they will prevent the group from adapting when necessary. This ideal might be approachable if boards are open to evaluating—or more important, simply *recognizing*—their routines.

Researchers have identified two main conditions under which routines are likely to change, and these can give us some insight into how boards might deal with them. First, routines are likely to change when the group encounters a novel situation.[13] Novelty, research shows, leads to higher level cognitive processes, which allows individuals to be open to new coding of the situation at hand. When boards encounter situations they "recognize," they are likely to move into the habitual behavior that has worked, whereas obviously "new" situations will lead to active assessment of what response is appropriate or likely to be effective. A question that has been harder to answer is *how* novel something must be in order to activate this openness to scanning the environment.

A second condition that can promote change is when the board or group must reassess its goals. This can occur either because of an unexpected failure to reach the goal or because changing conditions lead to a changed goal. Often goal reassessment takes longer to occur than one might think. This is because groups, like individuals and organizations, engage in what is called "satisficing." A particular level of performance or outcome is deemed "good enough," even if the performance does not reflect the group's best capability. Performance is just good enough to avoid very negative feedback. As a result, it often takes much more dramatic failure or catastrophic results to bring about a real goal reassessment. We see this happen on boards, of course, and by the time the discussion is taking place, many losses have occurred.

What Boards Can Do

The conditions described previously suggest several "interventions" that conscientious board members might accept:

1. Board leaders and directors who want to do effective board self-evaluations should ask the question, "What are our routines around

our most important activities?" Considering how the board tends to respond to conflict, such as how the board deals with problematic messages from management and similar issues, can reveal a lot about where the board might get stuck under certain circumstances.

2. Board leaders who are responsible for framing discussions can change the way in which discussions are run or votes are taken. For example, they might insist that members articulate concerns they have had but have not had the confidence to express. They can use the "six thinking hats" technique, described by Edward de Bono,[14] to scramble the thinking processes. For example, one board member can be asked to approach a problem neutrally, coldly focused on facts and figures ("white hat"), another can focus on creative thoughts ("green hat"), and a third can play a devil's advocate role ("black hat"). Or at least the board members can signal which "hat" they are wearing to help the board leader identify when one or more hats are being over- or underused. More simply, a leader can just switch discussion leadership styles, which might at various times include going around the table for comments, asking rhetorical questions, putting specific individuals "on the spot," or otherwise changing up the "process." Skilled board leaders can prevent the group from falling into a routine around important issues.

3. Boards can adopt a "metaroutine" whereby they consistently evaluate their process. An operations-level example of a metaroutine is total quality management (TQM). Meta routines like TQM put in place a process of reflecting on how well goals are being met and how consistent behaviors are with what is effective in the situation.

4. Finally, board leaders can adopt and exhibit a learning disposition that is open to process changes and comments, as well as dissent. Researchers find that it is hard for an individual to raise concerns about a routine when others are fully engaged in it. He or she may be dismissed or simply not understood by the others. In addition, they find that groups spend very little time discussing their own strategy for performing their work. Instead they make assumptions about what process is appropriate and speak almost exclusively about the substance of the task. Since groups are not naturally inclined, then, to see and challenge process routines, it is up to the group leader to make a space for this kind of reflection, learning, and change.

CHAPTER 7

Group Conflict

As noontime approached, Frank knew that he and his fellow Sym-Line Inc. board members still had one very important strategic issue to discuss before they could break for lunch. He was looking forward to a breather and a tour of the new company headquarters, but he tried to remain focused. Roy, the separate chairman of the board, had introduced this section of the board agenda, emphasizing that this discussion would involve an explicit decision point for the directors. The issue under consideration was a joint venture in a new but promising direction. It required a significant, up-front investment and careful negotiation with the potential partner organization.

As the CFO presented management's proposal, Jeff, the director sitting to Frank's right, interrupted with a series of questions. One of the more vocal directors, Jeff frequently interjected himself in the discussions like this, and his questions were always direct. Like always, each successive question drilled further beneath the surface. Gradually, Jeff revealed his skepticism about the proposed actions. Frank knew that he and others were on board with the current proposal, but they patiently listened as Jeff peeled back the layers to satisfy his own concerns. Eventually, Frank joined the discussion by asking Jeff what his predictions were about the potential consequences of the proposed partnering agreement. Although at this point Frank and Jeff were essentially in conflict with one another over the proposed plans and what they perceived to be the risks and benefits, they continued to focus on how each of them interpreted the situation, seeking to understand the heart of the disagreement. After a few exchanges, Frank, too, began to see Jeff's concerns, and he turned to ask management a few critical questions.

Soon the board members became focused on resolving the point of concern by adding some risk protections into the partnering agreement. Management agreed that the deal could still go forward if they negotiated for this compromise, and the board approved the proposal on that basis. Satisfied that they had collaboratively identified a conflict that wound up creating a different and seemingly better approach to the joint venture, the board broke for lunch. It was not unusual for them to have challenges and conflict emerge and to resolve it without hard feelings. Frank only wished his other boards were this good at working together.

In this book we focus on those aspects of group dynamics that are not driven simply by personality conflicts or the quirks of "difficult" group members. Overt conflict that arises in groups is often attributed to those factors. On some boards it can be observed that "Bill always disagrees with Marilyn" or "another meeting became divided and unproductive when Hank joined into the discussion." Focusing on the undesirability of conflict and on the role of individuals who create it is warranted because it reflects our personal experiences. However, it belies the fact that conflict is an inherent part of group life, and it can be beneficial to group performance.

Group conflict can be defined as "the process resulting from the tension between team members because of real or perceived differences."[1] For many years, group researchers focused on the numerous *negative* aspects of group conflict.[2] They showed that conflict undermines productivity by distracting members from the task at hand;[3] it decreases member satisfaction, which also indirectly impacts productivity;[4] and it produces antagonism between group members, which adversely affects the group's desire and ability to work together effectively in the future.[5]

However, as researchers began to tease apart different *types* of conflict, it became apparent that some kinds of conflict are not as detrimental as others, and some conflict can even be functional. The most frequently discussed types of conflict are task conflict and relationship conflict.[6] *Task conflict* includes disagreement about the "distribution of resources, procedures and policies, and judgments and interpretations of facts." *Relationship conflict* refers to conflict based on interpersonal style or values that people have.[7] A third type, *process conflict*, was also identified but has received less attention.[8] Process conflict refers to disagreements about how the group's task should be completed (e.g., who is responsible for what, how the group should proceed, how things should be delegated).[9]

A variety of studies focusing primarily on relationship and task conflict suggest that they have different consequences for group outcomes like effectiveness and member satisfaction.[10] Specifically, while relationship conflict is dysfunctional and nearly always detrimental to the group, moderate task conflict can be beneficial to the group.[11] Decision-making theorists point out that the diverse information and minority viewpoints contribute to effective decision making, a fact that may explain why task conflict seems to enhance group performance, particularly group decisions.[12]

The evidence regarding a possible positive relationship between task conflict and group outcomes is mixed, however (i.e., both for and against). Several studies showed that even task conflict was only beneficial in small amounts. As the amount of conflict increased, the benefits quickly dropped off and became detrimental.[13] One reason for this is that conflict—of any type—creates an extra cognitive load for the group members. Their abilities to process information are hampered as their attention becomes focused on the complexities of conflict rather than on filtering information directly relevant to the task.[14]

Despite all of this ambiguity about the good and the bad, today most scholars believe that conflict is not universally harmful for groups. All three kinds of conflict have been shown to be detrimental to groups, but not always. Rather, a number of contextual and situational factors influence the exact relationship that exists between conflict and group outcomes.[15] What factors have been identified?

Factors That Shape the Effects of Group Conflict

Four factors have recently been shown to affect how conflict plays out in groups. All four are also linked to the important group attributes of within-group trust and respect, positive motivation, cohesion, and empowerment.[16] In other words, the factors we will discuss diminish one or more of these group attributes. When we find them diminished, we are more likely to see that conflict will have a negative effect on the group.

The first factor that appears to affect how conflict affects groups is *resolution efficacy*. When groups have high resolution efficacy—a belief that they can succeed in resolving ensuing conflicts—the negative effect of some conflict on group performance is lower. This is true for process conflict in particular. In other words, having confidence in their ability to resolve future conflict reduces the damage that process conflict can do.[17]

A second factor, having *open norms about conflict*, is also effective in reducing the negative effects of process conflict. Having open conflict norms means that group members believe that it is acceptable and appropriate to raise and discuss differing opinions.[18] When these are the norms of the group, then the information and ideas about task and process that are brought to the table are more likely to have a positive effect on the group, in the form of better decisions and better interaction. Most research suggests that this is not true for discussing relationship conflict, however. Open norms about raising relationship conflict is not helpful and should be avoided.[19] Open norms about task and process conflict, in contrast, can actually prevent issues from becoming threatening and personal in a way that would produce relationship conflict.

Third, when relationship conflict includes a high degree of *negative emotion*—jealousy, hatred, anger, and frustration[20]—it is more likely to affect the group attributes of trust, respect, and cohesion negatively. This does not appear to happen with task conflict or process conflict.[21] Even when negative emotion occurs here, it does not necessarily affect the group performance or member satisfaction in a negative way. A likely explanation is that individuals are simply better able to separate themselves from negative emotions when they come up in a disagreement about task or process as opposed to some other circumstance.[22]

Finally, *norms that legitimate task conflict* have been shown to have a positive effect directly on the degree to which group members have high trust, respect, and cohesion. This is somewhat distinct from the previous three points. Conflict does not need to actually occur for us to see the positive (or less negative) effects of this factor. Simply having norms about discussing and treating task conflict openly has positive effects on the group.[23]

Because most work groups comprise a set of diverse individuals, differences in perspectives, experiences, and preferences are inevitable. But effective groups balance conflict with cooperation. These are the two fundamental components of group dynamics.[24] Conflict and cooperation are the push and pull of group activity, and both are essential to the group achieving its goals. Some argue that by moving through conflict, groups achieve the momentum they need to become collectively goal oriented and to achieve real cooperation and group activity. In this way, we see how conflict is essential to the very nature of group work.

Given this, we might wonder why individual group members are so averse to conflict. It is worth noting that individuals achieve benefits from maintaining a harmonious relationship with fellow group members. While it may not be the best thing for group process, it may be desirable to the individual. In this way, we could even construe conflict avoidance as a type of free-riding phenomenon, where individuals do not want to sacrifice their own personal relationships or comfort for the benefit or effectiveness of the group.

Group Conflict on Boards

If a board of directors does not experience conflict, it likely is not fulfilling its governance duties. On the other hand, a deadlocked or bitter group of directors is likely not achieving much either. By better understanding both the sources of conflict in groups and the conditions that influence conflict—in general and on boards specifically—boards may be able to reap the benefits of conflict while avoiding the potential detriments it can bring.

This chapter's focus on conflict also invariably brings out the very important relationship between the board and management—a relationship set up, in some ways, to produce conflict. Managing this potential conflict area effectively is critical to a board's overall effectiveness. We discuss it briefly at the end of this section.

The theoretical distinction between types of conflict does help to direct our attention toward certain aspects of boards or board meetings particularly important to group conflict. Leaving aside idiosyncratic personality difficulties, relationship conflict is most likely to emerge along the lines of perceived identity differences within a group. From the relational perspective, then, we must focus on those aspects of board membership that lend themselves to an us-versus-them framing among board members. These lines are uniquely shaped on each board, but some dimensions are likely to be common across most boards.

First, each board has at least one, if not more, "inside" directors, those who are also members of management. This creates a perceivable identity distinction between independent directors and inside directors. Another important dimension is tenure, particularly when a number of directors who have been on the board for many years are joined by a group of young or newer directors. Most boards we have seen have experienced some unplanned occurrence that eventually results in a perceived generational difference among the directors, which may reflect a difference in board composition before and after a particular incident in the company's history. The board of Medtronic Inc. at the time when Bill George took over, first as CEO and later also as chairman, provides a good example of a generational shift. In the 1990s, Mr. George was working with a board that had largely been around since the company's early days. As the governance and strategic environment changed for Medtronic, the board not only had to modernize its governance practices but also needed to populate the board with doctors and experts with relevant business and science backgrounds. The older directors, mostly from the Minneapolis area, were gradually replaced with a diverse group of younger directors. The transition was not easy, as the norms and expectations shifted; however, it was necessary given the growth of the company and given the changing governance demands. Perhaps these kinds of generational transitions will not happen as frequently going forward as boards have become more explicit, at least in their written governance principles, about retirement age and other efforts to stagger board membership.

On many boards distinctions in expertise are also apt to be drawn, such as between a subgroup of board members who have financial or industry expertise and those who do not. Finally, there is the relatively more visible distinction between "minority" directors—including women and ethnic minorities—and those who are male and Caucasian. A good board has diversity along all these dimensions, but it is important to recognize that the likelihood for both relationship conflict and the formation of subgroups grows as diversity[25] increases.

From a task perspective, multiple attributes of board work can cause conflict. One attribute is interdependence. The more interdependent a group is, the more likely it is both to experience task conflict and to have difficulty overcoming this task conflict in a positive way. Whether or not board work is truly interdependent is questionable. On the one hand, it is rare for one board member to rely on another board member in order to do his or her job. However, if the job is defined as the *collective* functioning of the board, then it is possible directors experience their task to be quite interdependent. This is a matter of framing. In our experience, some boards perceive their task to be a collective and cooperative one. On other boards, directors claim to be content as long as they, as individual directors, are doing what they can. Of course, the way a board goes about articulating and discussing its governance role can be critical to shaping this framing one way or another.

Finally, what boards do tends to be complex and ambiguous. Their job involves a high level of cognitive engagement. This kind of activity can make task conflict particularly hard to overcome.[26]

The Board and Management

Boards are subject to another condition that produces conflict—their interaction with another distinct group. Intergroup conflict is conflict that occurs *between* groups. One of the most startling and resilient findings in group research is that intergroup conflict can occur with almost no prodding. All that is needed is the perception that there are two distinct groups, even if those groups are randomly assembled.[27] Conflict occurs almost immediately when there is any sense of competition created between the groups. This usually happens when there is a scarce resource, something the groups must vie for. There may not be an obvious tangible resource for which management and the board compete. However, one can imagine the sensitivities that emerge over power—the power to define situations, the power over critical information, the power to make informed decisions, and even the power over board process, depending on whether or not the CEO and chairperson are the same individual. The board faces this intergroup tension and potential for conflict to an even greater degree than most work groups, because it does most of its work in the presence of and even in interaction with management.

With the exception of executive sessions and some committee meetings, directors are nearly always communicating simultaneously with each other and also across a very clear group boundary with management. Because interests between these two groups may sometimes be construed as diverging and because of the asymmetry of information that exists between them, their relationship is rife for skepticism, mutual testing, and conflict. We speak briefly to how this might be dealt with in the next section.

How to Avoid Destructive Conflict on Boards

In contrast with the ambiguity that surrounds task and process conflict, relationship conflict appears to be universally bad for group performance.[28] Its effects can be mitigated, but they will never be positive. Not surprisingly, task conflict is found to be less detrimental when it does not occur together automatically or frequently with relationship conflict. We must remember that conflict cannot be understood as an isolated incident but rather must be considered as a constantly evolving aspect of group life: performance can create conflict, conflict can affect performance, and one type of conflict can lead to another more detrimental kind of conflict (e.g., task conflict can bring about relationship conflict).[29] Whereas avoiding relationship conflict is critical, trying to shape the more inevitable task conflict into its constructive form can help boards be more effective.

Boards can endeavor to make conflict constructive in any of several ways:

1. Try to create strong within-group trust. Outcomes from task conflict tend to be more positive when groups experience strong within-group trust because members of such groups do not attribute malicious intent to each other's points, even when disagreeing. Group members are not inclined to construe a counterargument to be personally threatening in a way that leads to relationship conflict.[30] One way to enable trust is by creating strong norms about open disagreement and dissent and framing conflict as something

that is expected and appropriate to the group's process. When there is a group norm for openness, task conflict is more likely to produce its constructive effects. Related to this is developing over time the group's sense of efficacy in resolving conflict. This involves not leaving disagreement ignored and on the table without acknowledgment and some resolution, even if the resolution is to revisit the matter at a later date. Over time, groups that experience these kinds of positive outcomes develop confidence and a less avoidant, negative attitude toward conflict. This can keep conflict focused on task and process disagreements rather than on personal issues.

2. Create a climate of psychological safety. This leads to more positive outcomes from task conflict, including group learning and growth.[31] Psychological safety requires that group members believe they will not be punished for revealing ignorance or a mistake while working in the group.

3. Allow task conflict—the tension resulting from differences among team members with regard to judgments about or interpretations of the facts of the task—to become a routine part of discussion or decision making. When task conflict is produced deliberately and explicitly through the use of a devil's advocate, it is more likely to become productive for the group.[32] This can, over time, increase the group's sense of efficacy in dealing with conflict. And it is also not as likely to be taken personally.

4. Have the board leader establish effective group norms that define the ways in which dissent is solicited and conflict is treated once it surfaces. Research shows that when groups perceive that they have a common goal that requires cooperation, task conflict can be good for interpersonal relations and group performance.[33] In addition, when group members communicate their disagreements collaboratively rather than contentiously, the conflict is more likely to be experienced positively.[34] It is up to board leaders to create this kind of environment in their boards by the way they frame discussions and encourage dissent, even from people who might not be inclined to voice it. One way we have found that board leaders can create a collaborative and open environment is by periodically polling all directors to speak on a particular issue. Doing this as a way of sharing

information and perspectives gets all board members involved, with the implication that all are a legitimate part of the group's process. Some board leaders are very adept at anticipating conflict, either by having informal conversations before board meetings or simply by intuiting how directors might approach a certain point of discussion. Anticipating conflict enables them to frame it constructively immediately when it surfaces.

5. Diagnose conflict quickly and frame it constructively. By identifying points of disagreement and allowing them to surface, boards can keep task- and process-based conflict from evolving into relationship conflict. Boards that treat conflict as an inherent part of group process, rather than as a failure of the group or as frustrating side activity, are more likely to reap any benefits—and avoid the detriments—there might be from the conflict.

6. Identify and communicate *common goals*. When groups are competing with each other for resources or are faced with mistrust and disagreement, superordinate goals can create unison, cooperation, and even mutual trust over time. For a board, a superordinate goal can be clearly articulated as a governance role or an annual goal that gives it a common and stable sense of purpose. Several boards we have observed exhibited precisely such a collective goal (like "to be a leader in governance practice"), and it served as an anchor time and again when disagreements divided the board in important discussions.

7. Facilitate positive interactions between management and the board in meetings. In particular, a chairperson/CEO must adopt a nondefensive, open posture toward the board.

Conclusion

Conflict in board meetings is almost inevitable. Because most board members are adroit interpersonally and politically sophisticated, an outside observer might not even sense conflict on a board where in fact there is intense conflict. Erving Goffman's concept of "facework"—the work we do to save face, both our own and others'—is useful in thinking about how conflict happens in boards. Times of conflict are likely to produce precisely such behavior, efforts to make oneself and everyone else comfortable. This is true particularly if the members are highly attuned to keeping their positive image and must work together in the future. Groups engage in cooperative behavior to avoid conflict.[35] In an effort to keep interpersonal dynamics in order or to avoid confirming some conception of their group identity, individuals seek to avoid conflict. This does not mean that people privately agree, just that they are willing to act in a way that preserves the situation and interaction.[36] Rather than engaging in conflict, people may engage in impression management behaviors and cooperate with others to avoid overt conflict.

This final point simply illustrates why conflict can be so powerful in shaping behavior in boards, even when it does not surface. Conflict, just as much as cooperation, is fundamental to group life. But it need not be as detrimental as it often is.

CHAPTER 8

Power, Coalition Formation, and Politicking

In the early 1990s, UNI Storebrand, a large Norwegian insurance company, went bankrupt because of developments stemming from a failed hostile takeover bid for Skandia, a large Swedish insurance company. The takeover bid resulted in losses of billions of dollars for UNI Storebrand's shareholders, creditors, and customers. The autopsy of the event revealed that UNI Storebrand's CEO used multiple sources of power to convince the company's board of directors to approve the attempt. His power stemmed from his reputation and charisma; his position in some important power elites, such as the Norwegian "presidents club"; his participation in some interlocking directorates that helped him secure the support of other important Norwegian corporations; and his skillful exercise of influence with government politicians and bureaucrats. The influence over the government was aided by concentration of power; UNI Storebrand was the largest investor in the Norwegian financial market.

But the CEO was also manipulative in his exercise of power. He provided frequent briefings to government officials while being careful never to ask for permission to consummate the takeover, which was in violation of some Norwegian laws. But he gave the board members the impression that the government was supporting the takeover. Corporate management acted far ahead of board discussions, so that when the issue came up for discussion, the takeover proceedings had passed the point of no return, meaning that by the time the board got involved, multiple parties would suffer major losses if the takeover was not consummated. Before a critical shareholders' meeting, some shareholder activists were contacted and threatened so as to try to suppress their objections. And the CEO and board chairperson invited 800 employees to the meeting and instructed them to applaud whatever management said while reacting negatively to anything said by the opposition.

The ill-fated takeover bid had been discussed by the board 19 separate times, and it received unanimous support from the board each time.[1]

Power

Power is a major force in the functioning of groups and organizations. It is so important that Bertrand Russell, an influential 20th-century philosopher, called it "the fundamental concept in social science."[2] It greatly affects what gets done and how things get done in organizations. The effects can be for the better or the worse.

The terms *power*, *authority*, and *influence* are often used interchangeably. All three terms refer to the ability of one person (or group) to affect the behaviors, attitudes, or both of another person (or group) so as to produce outcomes in line with the person's (or the group's) perceived interests. Authority typically is the power vested in a position and is therefore exclusive to that position. But there are many sources of power and influence that are not exclusive to those in authority positions.

Power is not inherent to a person; it exists only in the context of relationships with others. Power is vested in someone by the dependence of others. By extension, power exercised in one particular situation may not be transferable to another situation. It is inherently dynamic.

People differ markedly in their abilities to create, maintain, and mobilize power. Some people are listened to intently when they talk, and others are not. Some board members actively build their power base through a range of activities outside the meetings in which they participate, building relationships, collecting information and perspectives through informal sources, and lobbying. But others do not. Unless something occurs to cause a loss of respect, an individual's power probably grows over time, as they become more familiar with the industry, the company, and the people involved in their work group.

Sources of Power

Power is difficult to observe directly. Rather, it is typically inferred and understood through analyses of its sources and consequences.

To understand how power can be used in dysfunctional ways, it is necessary first to understand how individuals develop power bases. The sources of power can be classified in many different ways. One influential book[3] identifies five main sources of power: personal, expert, informal network, formal (position), and past performance (track record). *Personal power* is derived from personal qualities, such as likability and charisma, or friendship. *Expert power* resides in a person's knowledge, experience, information, competence, and expertise in certain areas. Areas of expertise can range widely. It could be technical knowledge about the products or work processes themselves; or it could be social expertise, like having access to powerful friends. *Informal network power* is effected by associations in social networks and class elites. *Formal (position) power* stems from the position one holds. The position might entitle the person to some formal authority as well as control over rewards, punishments, and information provided. *Past performance power* is derived from a person's track record of success. People are inclined to listen to and follow others with a demonstrated record of success. The CEO of UNI Storebrand, described in the example presented at the beginning of this chapter, had all five sources of power available to him to use and misuse.

Sources of power can also be classified as direct or indirect.[4] *Direct power* exists where one person controls something that another wants. *Indirect power* exists when someone influences the agenda or meeting conditions, such as the venue and meeting format, that affect what individuals can and will do.

Inevitably, the individuals in a group—such as a board—do not have equal power either in total or in any specific decision-making area. As we discussed previously, power can be exercised in many different areas, such as in a business setting, finance, operations, marketing, and human resources. Individuals' expertise and records of success are likely to be quite different across these areas. However, perhaps more important, individuals' theoretical sources of power do not always translate into real power. It requires political savvy to use one's sources of power to actually get something done. Any individual manager or director may be lacking either the "will or the skill"[5] to exercise power in any given area.

Using Power

Individuals with both the will and the skill to influence others' behaviors can use any of many influence tactics. One article identified nine common influence tactics:[6]

1. *Rational persuasion* uses logical arguments and factual evidence.
2. *Consultation* requires involving the people who are being influenced in the decision-making process. It carries with it a willingness to modify the outcome to deal with concerns and suggestions raised.
3. *Inspirational appeals* arouse enthusiasm by appealing to a person's values, ideals, aspirations, feelings about success, or all four.
4. *Personal appeals* tap into a person's feelings of loyalty or friendship.
5. *Ingratiating appeals* seek to have the person think favorably of the requester, or at least to put them in a good mood, before the request is made.
6. *Exchange appeals* offer an exchange of favors, a promise to reciprocate a favor at a later time, or a promise to share the benefits.
7. *Pressure* uses demands, threats, or persistent reminders to influence the person to do what is wanted.
8. *Legitimation* seeks to establish the legitimacy of a request through a claim of the right to make it or a reminder that it is consistent with organizational policies, practices, or traditions.
9. *Coalition tactics* involve seeking the aid of others to persuade the target person to do something or using the support of others as a reason for the target person to agree to the request.

These tactics can be linked to the sources of power we have already discussed. Each source of power tends to be enacted using a certain limited set of tactics, as is shown in Table 8.1.

Table 8.1. Sources of Power Behind Some Common Examples of Influence Tactics

Influence tactic	Source of power				
	Personal	Expert	Informal network	Formal (position)	Past performance
Rational persuasion		x			x
Consultation		x			
Inspirational appeal			x		x
Personal appeal	x		x		
Ingratiation	x		x		
Exchange			x		
Pressure				x	
Legitimating tactics		x		x	x
Coalition tactics	x	x	x	x	

Outcomes of the Use of Power

There are three possible outcomes of an exercise of power through an influence attempt—commitment, compliance, and resistance. *Commitment* is where the person being influenced agrees with a request or decision and strives to carry out the request or to implement the decision effectively. *Compliance* is an outcome where the person is willing to do what is asked but is unenthusiastic about it. *Resistance* occurs when a person is opposed to carrying out the requests and decisions and actually resists performing the action.

Power in the Boardroom

Legally, boards have power de jure over management because of the legal authority that is vested in them. Legally, the board members themselves are equals. Their statutory powers and duties are equivalent because their responsibility is collective. In the eyes of most board members, boards are a small team of "colleagues, working together on a consensual basis and with collective responsibility for the direction of their organizations."[7]

The shareholders have the direct source of power—voting power over the board members. The board members' power is less direct because it is delegated to them by the shareholders. But it is real. The board members have legal obligations and the power to fulfill them. They can, for example, fire the CEO, who is the most powerful member of management.

But the board does not have unfettered power in the boardroom; management also has power over the board. Management has better knowledge of the company's day-to-day operations and the problems and opportunities facing the firm, and to a large extent, they control the channels that convey information to the board members. They also control resources—for example, analysts, internal auditors, staff experts—that provide expertise sources of power. Boards can ask for access to some of these resources, but there is a general reluctance to do so unless the perceived need is great. To gain greater power, directors must organize their efforts to gain greater de facto power.

The other important and interesting aspect of power in the boardroom is the balance of power within the board itself. All board members have been recruited to their position for some reason(s), and in this book we are assuming that those reasons exist and are legitimate. Those recruitment reasons each provide their own sources of power. If nothing else, board members usually have unique areas of relative expertise, such as a function (e.g., operations, finance, legal), a specific industry that is important because of supplier or customer relationships, or specific experience (e.g., mergers and acquisitions, initial public offerings).

In addition, one individual source of power that every board member has stems from the power of resignation or even the threat of resignation. When board members resign, regulators have to be informed, and people will ask why. If the explanation is disagreement with a board decision—such as regarding an acquisition, financing leverage, or executive compensation—public attention will be brought to that issue and the board's conclusions about it.

But, as stated earlier, power is not an attribute possessed by a person or a group of individuals in isolation. It is highly situational, and it is not static. Power is created and maintained or lost depending on the situations faced. Collective board powers tend to peak during crises, for example. Individuals' powers can also change over time as people build or demonstrate their competencies or, on the other hand, can become obsolete. And individuals' motivations and abilities to mobilize and use the power that they have may also vary markedly over time. For example, it has been shown that directors who are seeking additional board positions can improve their chances of being recommended for those positions by being relatively passive in their monitoring and control activities related to management decision making on strategic issues.[8] In this circumstance, which is not rare, the directors' will to confront top management and to exercise power over them is weakened.

The image that boards present to the outside world is that of a team, unified to help govern the corporation. But whereas the board members' legal responsibilities are equal, their powers are usually quite different. Board members' disproportionately large amounts of power can stem from any of many sources, including size of shareholdings, particularly visible or important areas of expertise, information, reputation, age, tenure, force of personality, or all of these. Just by watching, board observers are often able to get a good feeling as to who, in general, the most influential board members are.

As powers shift, as they invariably do, the relative balance of power within the complex social structure of the board can change dramatically over time and even in the short run depending solely on the specific issue being considered. These power shifts can have important effects on board functioning at any given moment. There is often a dominant coalition or clique, an "inner elite," that has disproportionate power in the boardroom. This power shapes who gets heard and why. The ability of certain individuals to build or influence these powerful coalitions is a major source of individual power in the boardroom.

Power can be exercised in both good and bad ways. Very often, and particularly with the most difficult types of decisions, board decision making depends on effective uses of power. Power is essential to the functioning of a board as almost nothing gets done without some person or group exercising power over another. Majority votes often depend on the effective exercise of power, the ability of one director, or a small group of directors, convincing others to vote with them. Board members need to build alliances—secure others' support in decision-making processes—to have an influence on board decisions. But power can also be exercised in bad ways. These dysfunctional exercises of power in the boardroom are the focus of the remainder of this chapter.

Dysfunctional Effects of Power in the Boardroom

The improper exercise of power in the boardroom can have huge, negative consequences, even bankruptcy, as the UNI Storebrand example described at the beginning of this chapter illustrates. Some improper exercises of power can lead to conflicts, which can have dysfunctional effects, as discussed in chapter 7. In the following sections, we discuss three other common, dysfunctional side effects of the exercise of power: (a) non–executive board member impotence; (b) inappropriate social influences on power, such as interlocking directorates; and (c) manipulative power games. These effects are not always independent, but they can be discussed separately.

An Example

A special conference call meeting of the compensation committee of the board of directors of Rainier Corporation was held on a Thursday morning early in February. The main agenda item was the discussion and possible approval of a proposed Change in Control Severance Agreement. John Anderson, Rainier's CEO/chairman, had asked to have the committee consider implementing such an agreement because Rainier had received an unsolicited offer of acquisition from a large Asia-based company. The issue was now urgent because Rainier management expected to receive the formal acquisition offer sometime in the next month or two.

After a series of meetings, Rainier's outside counsel drafted a severance agreement. The proposed agreement promised key executives lump-sum payments equal to three times the executive's highest annual salary plus bonus and some other benefits (e.g., continuing car allowance and medical coverage, outplacement services) in the event of a termination following a change in control of the company. In the event the payments exceeded the safe harbor amount set by the U.S. Congress, the payments would be "grossed up" to offset the excise tax that the executive would have to pay. (This excise tax is sometimes referred to as a "golden parachute tax.") The detailed agreement was sent to the compensation committee members in advance of the conference call.

Philip James, the CEO of a company on whose board Mr. Anderson served, was also the only compensation committee member who had had direct experience with such severance agreements, so he took the lead in organizing the discussion. Before the conference call, Mr. James called each of the other compensation committee members to answer questions they might have. Then on the call, Mr. James spoke first. He explained again that most companies had such agreements in place and why it was so important for Rainier to have one at this time. None of the other committee members voiced any reservations, and the severance agreement was approved unanimously.

Non–Executive Board Member Impotence

Up until recently, really the early 2000s, the checks on CEO power were relatively weak. Except in times of crisis, many boards of directors were relatively passive for many reasons, one of which was that the boards tended to comprise the CEO's friends and allies. However, stimulated by the collapse of the stock market in 2000 to 2001 and the major corporate scandals that were becoming public at about the same time, legislators, regulators, activist shareholders, and not coincidentally, boards of directors all sprung into action. Board members are now more likely to be recruited based on their expertise rather than on their ties with the chairperson, and boards are less likely to be passive.

One obvious manifestation of the transformation of corporate power was a series of firings of the heads of some of the world's best-known companies, including Disney, AIG, Morgan Stanley, Boeing, Hewlett-Packard, Bristol-Meyers Squibb, and Pfizer, just to name a few examples. The executive search firm Challenger, Gray & Christmas reported that U.S. firms fired or otherwise lost 1,484 CEOs in 2008, the most since the company began monitoring that market in 1999, more than double the figure in 2004. Formerly unchallenged CEOs found themselves under fire, often from their own handpicked boards. Clearly some of the boards that were forcing these firings, including those at AIG, Boeing, and Bristol-Myers Squibb, were reacting to the authority granted to them (or that they were reminded of) by new laws such as the Sarbanes-Oxley Act of

2002, by new stock exchange listing requirements, by pressure from the threat of lawsuits or new regulations, or by all these events combined.

Alan Murray, a columnist for the *Wall Street Journal*, believes that the balance of power between the CEO and the board, and hence the job of CEO, has permanently changed. He claims that well-respected corporate leaders like A. G. Lafley (Procter & Gamble) and Jeff Immelt (General Electric) now "govern" more than "rule." By that he means that they are more inclined to build alliances and support instead of giving orders and that they are paying attention to a broader range of stakeholders than ever before.[9]

Nevertheless, examples still exist where the non–executive board members have little power, such as in the Rainier Corporation (a disguised name) example described previously. Studies have shown that where the non–executive board members do not exercise their power, performance suffers.[10] The most common case where this phenomenon exists is the board that is dominated by a powerful chairperson who is often also the company CEO. Individuals who hold both the chair and CEO titles can potentially control the board meeting agendas. They can withhold necessary information to limit the board's interference in decision making, thereby retaining effective power. And they might not encourage the independent directors to play an active role. Some researchers have termed these board cultures as *minimalist*.[11] In these settings, non–executive directors have difficulty contributing to the success of the organization.

Even when they are not also playing the role of board chair, CEOs can exert an influence over the board because they play important roles in the selection and retention of board members. They can sometimes still stack the board with their friends and allies. This leads to the impression, and perhaps the reality, that the board members are serving merely at the pleasure of the CEO rather than fulfilling their independent oversight and evaluation roles.

One consistent finding is that board members in these settings of relative impotence find it easier to exert a negative influence—preventing things from happening rather than initiating new things.[12]

The standard solution to having a board dominated by a strong CEO/chairperson is to split the roles. In Germany the roles of the chairperson, as head of the supervisory board, and the CEO, who is head of the management board, are legally separated. But academic research focused on U.S. settings, where the separation of the CEO and chair roles is optional, has not found significant evidence of the performance advantages of such a separation.[13] Perhaps one reason for the lack of consistency in findings is that splitting the top role creates an inherent "recipe for friction."[14] It makes the relationship between the chair and CEO undoubtedly the single most important relationship in a corporation, and not all such relationships are effective.

Inappropriate Social Influences (Interlocking Directorates)

Sometimes directors form coalitions and exercise power based on their perceptions of what they need to do to be—or to remain—accepted into various social network ties rather than on their best rational judgments as independent board members. These social network ties can have many sources, including paternalism, friendships, and common educational, religious, or work backgrounds.

The existence of these social network ties, which contribute to high social cohesion on a board, has some advantages. On a highly cohesive board, board members are typically comfortable, and meetings will proceed smoothly, with relatively few distractions and relatively little confrontation. But social cohesion even between just two or a few members of a board can also have negative effects on board judgments and decision making and the power dynamic.

One good way to illustrate this point is to discuss the problem of *interlocking directorates*. These interlocks are the most prominent and tangible indicator of interfirm social network ties. Interlocking directorates exist where members of boards of directors serve together on the boards of more than one corporation. Such interlocks are common. A 2002 study by the Corporate Library, which monitors corporate governance practices, and *USA Today* found that nearly 2,000 boards and more than 22,000 U.S. board members are linked.[15] At that time, 11 of the top 15 firms had at least two board members who sat together on another board. Situations where CEOs sit on each other's boards are the kind of interlock that critics fear most.

Hard evidence about the dysfunctional effects of interlocking directorates is limited, but critics have provided some possibly troubling anecdotes. For example, the U.S. Securities and Exchange Commission won a case against Salomon Smith Barney (SSB) and former star research analyst Jack Grubman for research analyst conflicts of interest. Grubman had upgraded his rating on AT&T Corporation from Neutral to Buy. The concern was that this recommendation might have been influenced by the social relationships between the SSB and AT&T CEOs, who served on each other's boards. In the course of the investigation, it also came to light that prior to the upgrade, Sanford I. Weill, the co-CEO and chairman of Citigroup, asked Grubman to take a "fresh look" at AT&T, perhaps not coincidentally around the time he helped Grubman's children get into a desired nursery school.[16]

Another example: In 2000, communications giant Verizon, looking for ways to control health care costs, cofounded a lobbying group called Business for Affordable Medicine (BAM) and helped to recruit its corporate members. But Verizon left BAM in September 2002 because, said a Verizon spokesperson, the group sponsored legislation that the company opposed. What worries some people is that Verizon and drug-manufacturer Wyeth shared four board members, including the two companies' CEOs. Could the shared board members have pressured Verizon management to withdraw support for BAM? Wyeth denied this charge, although the company admitted that it sent several letters to Verizon expressing its disagreement with BAM.[17]

Interlocking directorates, and other social ties among board members, have the potential to be dysfunctional for several reasons. First, as illustrated by the previous anecdotes, interlocking directorates present the potential that board members might be too "cozy," placing their own social interests ahead of those of company shareholders. At a minimum, the coziness concentrates power in fewer hands than would otherwise be the case. At the extreme, the interlocks could contribute to illegal activities such as collusion and price fixing, but less important decisions can also be affected. For example, researchers found that interlock ties are associated with the introduction of "poison pills."[18] They explained that heavily interlocked directors are the corporate elite, and poison pills are an innovation designed to protect this elite from a practice—takeovers—that they view as dangerous.

Even if the decision-making realities are not affected by the inter-locked directorates, the interlocks, or other social ties if they are visible, can present perceptual problems. The mere existence of the interlocking directorate gives outsiders the impression that such problems could exist.

Second, when board members sit on multiple boards together, they tend to develop a common way of thinking. Highly linked boards are likely to engage in less independent thinking, and the company is more likely to be blindsided by changes they did not see coming. For example, the interlocks on bank boards are known to be particularly high.[19] It is not implausible to suggest that these interlocks could have contributed to blinders leading to the major crisis felt in the financial services industry in 2008 to 2010.

Third, interlocking directorates might contribute to or exacerbate situations of conflict, which, as discussed in chapter 7, are nearly inevi-table in the boardroom. They can lead to directors' motives being ques-tioned because the interlocking directorates lead to the perception that decisions are based on social concerns more than on expertise, logic, and objective analysis.

The general problem—of which interlocking directorates provide a prominent example—is inappropriate social influences on decision-making processes. Inappropriate social influences may stem originally from any of many board member commonalities, including back-grounds; race; and university, religious, and social club affiliations.

Manipulative Power Games

In any group, including boards of directors, some group members accept that they have less than equal power. Others do not. And some individu-als have a natural desire for power. They want to assert more authority over the other group members. Then once they have gained power, they will tend to defend their sources of power. Often others will fight back, leading to a power struggle.

Do power struggles occur in the boardroom, even if the board is composed solely of mature, competent individuals, all with congenial personalities? Clearly the answer is yes. There are many examples of power struggles at the board level, including some prominent ones such as that between Steve Jobs and John Sculley at Apple Computer and the board struggle at Hewlett-Packard in the Carly Fiorina era.

Power is often exercised through politics and strategizing. Those who endeavor to have their course of action be the chosen one must have more power than those who prefer a different course of action. Sometimes they must take steps to build their sources of power in order to increase their influence. So power struggles, which can involve politicking and coalition formation, are essential processes in organizations of any size. Power struggles have inevitable costs, but they can be tolerated if everyone is fighting fairly. Most power struggles involve legitimate power-building and power-maintenance activities, such as logical persuasion and coalition building. Sometimes, however, particularly where power is especially important to a particular individual, there is the potential that that person might build or use his or her power unfairly. Such misuses of power are probably relatively common in business and corporate settings where individuals tend to be aggressive and competitive and, some critics would say, relatively greedy and prone to unethical behavior.

One researcher who conducted a multiyear corporate anthropological study found that power-related struggles and infighting were so common that company executives had names for common behaviors.[20] An *ambush* (also called a *bushwhack* or a *cheap shot*) was a "cover action to inconvenience an adversary." *Blindsiding* was "an intentional and surprising public embarrassment by one executive at another's expense." An *outlaw* was "an executive who handles conflict in unpredictable ways but who is regarded as especially task competent." In some cases, such maneuverings would result in a *meltdown*—"a physical fight between executives."[21]

Manipulative power games of these and other types can also take place in the boardroom. Board members' processes of obtaining, retaining, and using power are not always attractive. Infighting can incur the cost of significant resources, and people often get upset. But upsetting some people might be just what is needed to overcome paralysis and inaction. Sometimes the most aggressive, even sleaziest, individuals are among those who accomplish the most. But sometimes these manipulative political processes get out of hand and cause very harmful effects.

Eisenhardt and Bourgeois considered the effects of political behaviors such as the degree of full disclosure of information in meetings, the formation of insurgency groups, internal and external alliances, withholding information, agenda control, and provision of attempts to co-opt or lobby key executives.[22] They found that the greater the use of these political behaviors, the poorer the firm's financial performance. The reasons they gave for this result included time wasted engaging in politics, restricted information flow, and distortion of people's perceptions.

At their worst, power games—things done to extend a board member's sphere of influence—can involve morally questionable or even illegal activities. In the morally questionable category are actions such as exercising inappropriate favoritism, hiding important information from other board members, and in the case of a board chair, keeping important issues off the board agenda or not allowing adequate time for discussion. In the illegal category are many forms of corruption, such as lying, kickbacks, bribery, and blackmail.

Exercising Power Without the Dysfunctional Side Effects

Boards cannot prohibit their members' use of power. In fact, the exercise of power in the boardroom is not bad; it is inevitable and necessary. It plays numerous important roles in the boardroom. Indeed, "governance" is all about the exercise of power. Board members should try to convince others that their ideas are good and that their perspectives are correct. But some exercises of power are dysfunctional. How power is mobilized and used in and around the boardroom has major impacts on the choices made by the board, and it can have effects that go beyond those choices.

What are the conditions, processes, and abilities that contribute to the development and proper, rather than dysfunctional, exercise of power—particularly by part-time, non–executive board members? Regulations, such as the U.S. Sarbanes-Oxley Act of 2002, can help emphasize the legitimacy of the role of the board and its independent members. But even then the part-time board members have to construct their own power base from which to exercise influence. The following point to the functional exercise of power by the board and its members:

1. Clearly the chair plays an important role in shaping the board norms and culture. A good chair should govern instead of rule. A good chair must demand clear and regular communications from the CEO and others on the top management team to ensure that the board is well informed. The chair plays a major role in setting the agenda, in determining the extent to which the board members are informed and contributing to the agenda, in making sure organizational policies are open and fair, in encouraging equity and collaboration, and in allowing and encouraging every member to exercise their initiative, to express their ideas, and to fulfill their responsibilities. Board members who perform well can and should be praised openly and personally. Thus, the chair can be instrumental in making sure the board is not a minimalist board. CEOs who resist these steps might have to be replaced, or at least steps will have to be taken to reduce the CEO's influence. This is a major cause behind the call for separation of the chairperson and CEO roles.

2. Some checks and balances should be implemented to counter the power of dominant groups or those that might become dominant in harmful ways. One method involves the recruiting of more diverse members to the board rather than recruiting solely from the "old boy network." Diversity reduces the social influences that can both blind the board and create an inner, dominant power clique. But a more independent board is not necessarily the best control against inappropriate uses of power because very independent boards are generally less knowledgeable and less engaged.

3. Committee structures share and devolve power to smaller groups of directors. Using committees addresses the information source of power because it reduces the information overload problem. Committees also allow individual directors to meet more often and focus more intensively on critical problems, thus managing the information overload problem before the general board meetings.

4. If the CEO, anyone else on the top management team, or any member of the board is found to use manipulative devices to influence

board activities, they should be replaced immediately. Those at the top of the organizational pyramid must behave with the highest moral standards.

The most effective boards function as high-performance teams. Members have defined roles to play. They complement each other. They trust each other but are also not reluctant to challenge each other and to engage directly with senior managers on the critical issues. They are proactive, taking steps to ensure that they are well informed on the most important issues. And they exercise their power in positive ways, through persuasion and the building of alliances, not by deception and bullying.

CHAPTER 9

Group Productivity Losses

We usually don't finish everything on our agenda. I plan the schedule carefully and try to keep us on schedule. But almost everything seems to take longer than it should. Then, toward the end of our scheduled time, guys are looking at their watches, worried about whether they are going to catch their planes, and some have already left. So we rush through some agenda items, and we almost always decide to defer some others to the next meeting.

—Lead independent director of a NASDAQ-listed medical devices company

The problem illustrated in the above quotation could be caused by lack of discipline from the leader in keeping the meeting on schedule, but it could also be caused by poor group productivity. Working in groups can enhance or hurt productivity, depending on the task and situation. Working with others can sometimes cause people to work harder, to think more carefully, to learn more, and to have new ideas stimulated than does working alone. Groups can, indeed, produce more than the sum of what the individuals in the group could contribute individually. Generally, though, productivity gains are relatively rare and usually modest.[1]

In most groups, productivity *losses* are thought to be much more common than are the gains, and their effects are larger. Groups often perform quite inefficiently. Perhaps everyone has been in a group that has not lived up to its full potential. For many tasks, and particularly the types of tasks that boards of directors engage in, groups often fail to operate as efficiently as might be expected given the capabilities of the individuals involved. The productivity losses cause the groups to consume more resources—in the boardroom, particularly, time—than should be needed to accomplish their tasks. That, in turn, can have deleterious effects on both the quantity and quality of work done, as might be occurring in the example described above. Boards (and other working groups) fail to do everything they would like to do, or they rush through everything they must accomplish and quality suffers as a result. There are two basic causes of productivity losses in groups.[2] One is the decline in motivation, which was discussed in the social loafing section of chapter 2. The other is commonly referred to as *coordination losses*. These occur when the individual group members' responses are not combined optimally or when one group member's activities interfere with those of the other group members. In this chapter we discuss the causes of these coordination losses, the situations where they are more or less severe, and what might be done to alleviate them.

The Meaning of Productivity

Productivity is an indicator of the efficiency with which an individual, group, or organization uses its resources (inputs) in doing whatever it aims to do (outputs). Depending on the group, the outputs could be products, services, or the completion of specific tasks that might result— for example, in a boardroom setting—in a solution or a decision.

This productivity definition is easy to apply where both the inputs and outputs are easy to measure, which is mostly likely in highly routinized settings. For example, assume that in an automobile repair shop setting it takes a knowledgeable, energetic worker working in ideal working conditions one half hour to do an automobile oil change. This half hour of time spent per oil change is a *theoretical ideal* performance standard that is useful for aspirational purposes. If it takes more than one half hour to do an oil change, the operation is said to be "less than perfectly efficient" in the use of time. The inefficiency could be caused either by the working conditions or by the worker's knowledge or behaviors. *Partial productivity measures* can also be calculated for the use of other factors of production, such as space or power. If all the factors of production can be measured and aggregated on the same measurement scale—such as dollars—then a measure of *total productive efficiency* can be calculated as total value of outputs divided by total value (cost) of inputs.

Also useful as a comparison standard is a *practical ideal* that takes normal working conditions into consideration. The practical ideal reflects what a good worker realistically can be expected to accomplish. This practical ideal might make allowances for employee vacations, breaks, fatigue, and sick leaves and maybe even the possibility of relatively rare events, such as power failures and natural disasters. When using a theoretical ideal, workers will always fail to achieve the ideal. But with a practical ideal standard, it is possible for some of the best workers to perform at 100% efficiency or, in some cases, even better than that.

Group Productivity

Can these definitions of productivity be applied to a group's work setting? It can, but only if performance (output) can be measured and a performance standard, either theoretical or practical, can be identified for the group's outputs and inputs. Without identifying a performance standard, it is impossible to conclude definitively whether the group is achieving, exceeding, or falling short of the expected level of performance.

Productivity standards can be developed and compared with actual outputs for some types of group tasks. Where group tasks are *additive*, a good group performance standard can be determined and defined as the aggregation of what the individuals in the group could accomplish. With such tasks, the group members are working independently, so the group output is just the sum of the outputs of the individuals in the group. Continuing the automobile repair shop example, assume the repair shop has a group of workers assigned to do oil changes. The per-unit theoretical ideal would remain the same—one half hour per oil change. Thus, the ideal number of oil changes for the oil-change group to complete would increase linearly with the number of workers in the oil-change area of the shop.

Additive tasks may be either *unitary* or *divisible*. Unitary tasks are accomplished holistically, as would be the case if the automobile repair shop's policy was to have a single person complete the entire oil change. Divisible tasks can be divided into subtasks, each of which could be undertaken by a different person. This would be the case if the oil-change tasks (e.g., remove and dispose of the used oil, add the new oil) were done by different workers. Useful performance standards, and hence productivity measures, can be calculated for all additive tasks whether they are unitary or divisible.

Some other group tasks are completed when just a single person in the group completes it. These are referred to as *disjunctive* tasks. The theoretical ideal for disjunctive tasks is often difficult to ascertain, but it is probably close to what can be accomplished by the group's most capable member. In general, productivity in performing disjunctive tasks is higher when the group comprises the more competent individuals. That competence increases the probability that the group includes at least one person who can complete the task, such as solving a problem, and it decreases the expected time for completion of the task. Disjunctive task productivity will also increase with the size of the group because it is more likely that a larger group will contain someone who is able to complete the task and complete it more quickly.

A third type of group task requires everyone in the group to complete the task. These are called *conjunctive* tasks. In the social psychology literature, the most commonly cited example of a conjunctive task is that of a group of mountaineers attempting to scale a peak. Conjunctive task productivity is affected by group composition and size. However, it is usually most adversely affected by the competence of the weakest member of the group. Larger groups are more likely to have one or more weak members.

The final category of group tasks encompasses what are usually referred to as *discretionary tasks*. With these tasks, the groups decide how to accomplish the task. Since their approaches can be idiosyncratic, discretionary task productivity can be assessed only on a relative basis, by comparing the output of like groups performing the same tasks. Some groups will be shown to be more productive than others. But such comparison possibilities do not always exist.

These group-task categories are not exclusive. Tasks can be, for example, both disjunctive and discretionary. The categories are, however, distinguishable, and they are useful because they help us think about commonalities among certain types of tasks.

Tasks in the Boardroom

Can these task categories be related to the activities performed in the boardroom? To a large extent, they can. Boards perform many types of tasks. They review decisions proposed by management and make judgments about their efficacy. Some of these judgments, when in technical areas such as accounting, information technology, or engineering processes, are heavily influenced by one or just a few board members who, for reasons of education or experience, might be considered the most knowledgeable.

The other board members generally defer to these experts, so these types of reviews are most like disjunctive tasks. Reviewing documents such as contracts and regulatory filings might also be considered as examples of disjunctive tasks. As soon as one competent board member has reviewed the document carefully, that task is often deemed to have been completed.

Additive tasks are relatively rare in the boardroom, but they do exist. Completion of board self-evaluation questionnaires is an example of a unitary, additive task. Each board member works independently in completing a questionnaire. Still other tasks might be broken down with specific pieces assigned to different board members. An example might be a review of documents such as a 10-K report or a series of contracts. When individual board members are assigned to review only a portion of the total reviewing task, this overall assignment is a divisible, additive task.

In boardroom settings, conjunctive tasks are rare. It is generally not necessary to ensure that weak board members complete any given task.

Many board processes fall in the discretionary category because the discussions are largely free form, not following any routine. The processes involve creativity, complex trade-offs, and ambiguity.

Some board tasks, such as development or evaluation of business strategies, involve multistep processes. They often start with a collective idea-generation element, such as brainstorming, as board members search for viable approaches they can analyze further. Brainstorming is an additive task. Then the reviews require some or considerable discussion to evaluate the ideas. This element of the group process is designed to move the board members, who might start with a diverse set of perceptions and preferences, to agreement on a consensus choice for the group. These discussions probably do not follow a regular pattern, so they would fall in the discretionary task category.

As mentioned previously, productivity in accomplishing discretionary tasks cannot be measured with any precision. Thus, there are no studies that say, for example, that the board of directors of ABC Corporation is operating at only 79% efficiency, and rankings of board productivity do not exist. However, some productivity extremes are identifiable; it is possible to make judgments about things that will make a board more or less productive, and it is possible to make suggestions to improve board productivity in various situations.

Productivity Losses in Groups

Consider the following example:

> In late 2008, Beachwear Inc., a regional retailer of casual fashion apparel and accessories for teens and young adults, was facing a crisis. Sales were down sharply, and competitors were encroaching on all fronts. The company's very existence was threatened. Jonathan Adler, chair of Beachwear's board, knew that the board had to take action. While management was considering a range of alternatives, Jonathan thought that the board might also be able to provide some useful ideas. He was considering two options. One was to have the board members generate ideas on their own for presentation at the next board meeting, which was coming up next month. The other option was a group "brainstorming" session at the board meeting.

In situations like the example described here, most people instinctively would choose the group brainstorming option. There is a widespread, intuitive belief that interactive, face-to-face groups generate more creative ideas than do *nominal groups*, equal numbers of individuals working in isolation. The rationale behind this belief is that creative ideas and new associations can be stimulated by the interaction among group members.[3]

Interestingly, however, this belief is generally not true, at least for this kind of creative group activity. Many psychological studies conducted over several decades have shown exactly the opposite. Research on creativity, for example, has shown that when the nonredundant ideas of a group of individuals working independently is compared with the ideas of a same number of similar individuals working as a group, the individuals working separately produce both more ideas and higher quality ideas.[4] The productivity loss in the group activity is significant. The losses are found consistently in groups of three members or larger, and they increase with group size. Group interaction seems to inhibit rather than stimulate creative idea generation.

The most widely cited model of group productivity is that of Steiner.[5] Steiner's law of group productivity is that the actual productivity of a group is equal to the potential productivity minus losses due to faulty processes. Processes are the ways in which the group members transform their resources into a group product. In Steiner's model, process can only have a negative effect on productivity. The decades of research that followed the publication of Steiner's model have generally supported this conclusion—groups generally fall short of productivity standards that might reasonably be set for them.[6]

Causes of Productivity Losses

There are four main causes of productivity losses in groups. One is a motivational problem. Since it is difficult or impossible to isolate individual contributions when individuals are working in a group, individuals cannot be held accountable for their contributions or lack thereof. This lack of accountability can lead to the free-rider effect, or social loafing, as discussed in chapter 2.

A second potential problem is a self-censoring behavior that occurs naturally when people work together. This phenomenon is sometimes called *evaluation apprehension*. Individuals working in a group often fail to mention some ideas that might be particularly creative because they fear the ideas might be judged strange, bizarre, or antisocial. They censor themselves because they fear their ideas might be judged as of low quality.

A third problem is called the *social matching effect*. The best performers in a group often reduce their contributions to match those of their less capable team members. This might be done because either they do not want to stand out from the group or they judge that they can be full contributors with less effort.

Finally, there is a problem, which might be generally the most serious,[7] that is called *production blocking* or *cognitive interference*. It results from the normal process used in group decision-making settings, that is, an implicit rule that only one person speaks at a time. Since group members have to share the floor with their colleagues, their production of ideas is somewhat blocked by the other group members. Because individuals in groups can only speak one at a time, ideas cannot be verbalized the instant they occur. Individuals must wait for their turn to speak. In the period of delay that individuals face between idea generation and expression, they tend to get distracted, and their ideas are often forgotten or suppressed, or the discussion takes a turn in a way that makes their idea difficult to fit in to the new context of the discussion.

A number of experiments have been designed to test for the existence of production blocking.[8] In one experimental condition, the one-person-talking-at-a-time rule was strictly enforced. In the other condition, subjects were told that they did not have to take turns talking. The results suggested that production blocking was, indeed, a major cause of productivity losses in this setting.

A series of follow-up experiments was designed to explore the underlying causes of production blocking in more detail.[9] One hypothesis suggested that participants working in groups do not have enough time to express their ideas because the speaking time has to be shared among group members. The experiment designed to test this hypothesis found that the overall speaking time was not important. The most significant losses occurred when ideas could not be expressed soon after they were generated.

Several other experiments were designed to see if the speaking order made a difference. Speaking in high-level groups like corporate boards is generally not highly controllable. The first group member who speaks usually has the floor. Other group members have to monitor the discussion to find an opening to talk. This monitoring activity could distract them from generating ideas. So the experiments tested the effects of having a predictable waiting time (taking turns in a fixed order) or a controllable waiting time (sign up on a speaking list). But this variation in setting had no effect on productivity. In either case, after group members generated an idea, if they could not voice it immediately, the effect was the same. They had to rehearse it in memory continually in order not to forget it. Allowing note taking improved performance slightly, but only when instant communication was not possible.

One major conclusion of this series of experiments is that waiting times is the major cause of productivity losses in brainstorming groups. Group members have to multitask. They have to listen, they have to generate useful ideas, and they have to monitor the discussion to determine if and when there is an opening for them to present their idea. These requirements seem to overload the cognitive abilities of at least most people. The disjointed nature of most group discussions seems to interfere with individuals' abilities to get a productive train of thought started, or at least maintained.

Any or all these causes of productivity losses can be present in any group setting, but some group characteristics can make them more or less salient. One important factor is group size. As group size increases, the potential for production blocking increases because the airwaves become more crowded. There are more people taking up speaking time and more people who can interrupt the discussions.

Boardroom Remedies to Productivity Losses

Since it is usually difficult to determine reasonable performance standards for group tasks of the types that corporate boards most often engage in, little hard evidence about boardroom productivity exists. But some theories about group productivity can be applied to the boardroom setting. Researchers and consultants have used these theories to develop techniques designed to help groups avoid coordination-type productivity losses. The techniques address one or more of the underlying causes of the productivity losses. Some of them focus on the individuals; some focus on the task, or perceptions of the task; and some focus on improving group processes. All the techniques affect how group members interact with each other as they perform their tasks.

Team Development

Some productivity-improvement techniques fall under the rubric *team development*. Team development training is designed to improve the group members' decision-making, communication, and interpersonal skills. It can focus on problem identification, sensitivity training, role analysis, and methods of coping with time pressure and other types of stress.[10]

For example, productivity in performing disjunctive tasks can be improved if groups better recognize the various areas of relative expertise of their members. With this knowledge, they can better determine whom to rely on to provide certain kinds of advice. Expertise reveals itself in many ways. Directors may know each other's backgrounds, or they may observe each other's knowledge and behavior in meetings. But recognizing areas of knowledge and expertise can also be enhanced with some formal interventions. These might include explicit instructions for sharing task information, performance feedback, or group exercises that provide opportunities for members to learn more about each other's competencies.[11]

Team development can also involve training group members to follow certain discussion or decision-making rules that have been shown to have beneficial effects. For example, members can be usefully reminded to stay focused on the task, to avoid talking in pairs, and to avoid monopolizing the session.

Process Improvements

Boards' *process improvements*, some employing technology, can also be made to minimize the productivity-loss problem. For example, nonverbal processes that force or allow individuals to make their contributions in writing or electronically rather than vocally in face-to-face interactions can reduce production blocking because they allow group members to contribute their ideas without interruption.[12] If the contributions are made anonymously, the evaluation apprehension problem is also minimized. Computerized brainstorming groups have been shown not to suffer productivity losses. They can even outperform nominal groups when the groups are relatively large (more than nine members), which demonstrates the stimulating effects of exposure to others' ideas.[13]

The social matching problem can be minimized by raising feelings of competition among group members or by providing special recognition to the group members who contribute the most. Praising an individual board member for finding the most errors, or the most significant error, in a draft 10-K report, for example, will create positive intrinsic motivational benefits for that apparently particularly knowledgeable, perceptive, or careful board member reviewer.

Another kind of process improvement, based on research by Mankins, is to adopt a set of "rules" or standards against which all decisions are measured. This keeps discussions focused and makes substantive points to be addressed more identifiable and clear.[14] One such set of standards is used by Barclay and includes three basic tests. All decisions must be "fact based, alternatives driven, and consequential." What specific rules are used will vary by organization, but having them may be an important guide to making efficient use of time and resources.

Board Leadership

Improving *board leadership* can also be important in minimizing the group productivity problem. An effective leader, who might be either the board chair or a trained facilitator brought in from outside, can minimize the production blocking/cognitive interference and evaluation apprehension problems. It is generally impossible to orchestrate board meetings so that the board members do not interrupt, or otherwise distract, each other. But trained discussion leaders can sometimes give group members task-relevant information that properly frames their task, and perhaps simplifies it.[15] The process improvements might involve having the board consider issues sequentially to minimize the disjointed, sometimes chaotic, nature of some board discussions, thus reducing the board members' cognitive loads. Skilled board leaders might also decide that for certain tasks and at certain times it is functional to allow for some forced breaks to allow board members to think in silence, without their BlackBerrys, to collect their thoughts. And when needed, skilled leaders can motivate the group members to focus, to stay on task, or to dig deeper into the creative thoughts in their brains to develop action alternatives.

Conclusion

Most working groups, including corporate boards, suffer productivity losses that are difficult to measure precisely but are thought to be significant. All groups, even those containing the right number and mix of highly qualified individuals, all with congenial personalities, are less productive than we might expect them to be. They suffer both the motivational problems discussed in chapter 2 and the coordination problems discussed in this chapter. The coordination problems are caused by the inherent requirement of accomplishing tasks through the joint efforts of people who do not all think alike and must communicate and debate before completing their tasks.

Minimizing these losses is obviously important. More productive boards accomplish more, are more likely to accomplish their tasks effectively, and consume less of their members' valuable time. Fortunately, many of these productivity problems can be minimized, if not eliminated. Recognizing the problems and understanding their underlying causes are the necessary first steps.

CHAPTER 10

Conclusion

When something major goes wrong at a corporation, some, if not most, of the blame is eventually laid at the feet of the board of directors. For example, before and even during the financial crisis of 2008 and 2009, General Motors (GM) was generally seen as having a "blue-chip" board that comprised many highly competent, very experienced board members who were apparently taking their jobs seriously. But after the financial crisis necessitated a GM bailout by the government, Steven Rattner, the federal government's appointed "car czar," concluded that "if ever a board needed shuffling, it was GM's, which had been utterly docile in the face of mounting evidence of looming disaster."[1] How can such a seemingly high-quality board apparently have failed so miserably?

The GM example is not an isolated one. Studies of the boards of other companies that have had dramatic failures, including Enron, WorldCom, Tyco, and Lehman, have not found broad patterns of incompetence or corruption.[2] These boards, by most objective indicators of best practice, including board size and composition, meeting attendance, makeup of committees, financial literacy, and ethics and conflicts of interest policies, appeared to be near-model boards. But these boards seem to have fallen victim to some blind spots and monitoring and decision-making pathologies that caused, or at least failed to prevent, catastrophic failures. In some cases, the board members apparently had limited knowledge of what was actually going on in the companies they were supposed to serve, and in others they were blindsided by the effects of factors that they seemingly could not even envision. Tyco's directors, for instance, did not know that the CEO and CFO were giving themselves year-end bonuses months before the end of the year. The Enron board approved a system in which Enron's CFO, who also served as head of an outside entity that was doing business with Enron, was effectively allowed to negotiate with himself. On the Enron and Tyco boards, directors consistently deferred to company executives instead of challenging them. They discouraged debate and disagreement instead of cultivating it.

Effective board processes must not be circumvented. Individual directors must voice their grievances, be critical consumers of information they receive from management, and be active participants in shaping their own norms and processes.[3] Smart group decisions emerge out of discussions and disagreement, not rapid consensus. But on too many corporate boards, dissent is still seen as either superfluous or harmful. The blind spots created by group dynamics are not well appreciated by many, probably even most, boards. Thankfully the catastrophic problems that occurred at the giant corporations like Enron, Tyco, Lehman, and GM are rare. However, similar but less severe problems are occurring in the boards of many, if not most, corporations. The risk is always present. Through awareness and consideration of how board process may exacerbate or mitigate certain elements of group behavior, the problems and the damages they cause can be better anticipated and also minimized.

In this book, we have argued that board failures are nearly inevitable, even in the boards that seem perfectly put together. Group dynamics create conditions that can cause many types of blind spots, biases, and other pathologies to proliferate in the boardroom. The discussions in the prior chapters describe a large number of things that can go wrong in board meetings. The differences among them are subtle. When a board does not tolerate dissent, is it groupthink? Is it simple normative pressure? Is it abuse of power or politicking among factions? The answer is, it depends. In this book we have provided the theoretical background that can help directors diagnose a variety of group pathologies. Many of their observable consequences may be the same—silence, conformity, inefficiency—however, the set of underlying causes for each pathology is unique.

One aim of this book has been to give directors the understanding to identify *symptoms* of dysfunctional group behavior. We have covered the following: Even the most accomplished and qualified board members are prone to "loaf" in board settings. All are susceptible to group conformity pressures. Directors, like members of all groups, tend to spend most of their time discussing information everyone already knows. They will not raise individual concerns with the group, which then suffers from pluralistic ignorance. Boards tend to make more extreme decisions than the directors individually want to make. They may display the perception of invulnerability and pressure for group loyalty characteristic of group-think. Boards fall into routines and fail to question whether they are still appropriate to the situation they face. They allow conflict to become emotional and destructive rather than useful. And, finally, they are vulnerable to divisive and abusive uses of power.

A second aim of this book, of course, has been to provide the theories that will help boards to *diagnose* the causes of their symptoms. When directors consider the underlying factors—the functioning of the board, the combination of circumstances and behaviors that characterize the board process—they can decide how best to address the pathologies their boards face.

In this final chapter we attempt to draw out some themes that have emerged from this work. First, we point to a set of tensions that are nearly inevitable in boardroom settings. These tensions require striking a balance—recognizing that some board characteristics bring both good and bad effects, depending on which group behavior is being considered. Next we summarize some of our most salient suggestions, those that can help minimize the effects of more than one pathology. Finally, we provide some cautions. Even the best boards, for example, those of the right size and composition, are not perfect. There are inherent limits as to what can be expected of them. Regulators and society must understand these limitations and consider them when they institute other forms of governance and oversight.

Unavoidable Board Tensions

What makes management of board dynamics so difficult is that some of the advice that we have provided in the prior chapters is conflicting. We argue for more of one thing in one chapter and for less of it in another chapter. This is because of some inherent tensions in groups and in boards specifically. Boards must find a near-optimum level for factors that provide diminishing returns, and they must strike a balance between factors that can ameliorate one type of negative effect while producing another. The following are some of the important balances that must be struck.

Some Social Cohesion, But Not Too Much

Social cohesion, created by similarities in board members' backgrounds, experiences, or both, has some advantages. It makes the board meetings more pleasant to attend. It also tends to reduce, if not eliminate, the power struggles and bickering that paralyze some boards.

However, high social cohesion is also dangerous. It can suppress discussion and dissent. It can enhance the formation of stultifying habitual routines, the shared information bias, and various forms of dysfunctional conformity, such as polarization and groupthink. It can also contribute to or exacerbate situations of conflict if it is perceived that the social ties are affecting decisions more than are information, logic, and objective analysis. All these effects can lead to bad outcomes.

How, then, can the board address this tension? One way is to encourage a particular *type* of cohesion. *Task* cohesion tends not to be as loaded with social pressure and politics as does *social* cohesion. It can bring some of the benefits of social cohesion, without causing the detriments. Task cohesion refers to the forces of cohesion or of keeping the group together that exist because of the tasks in which the group is engaged.[4] Individuals are attracted to the group's task and therefore want to remain tightly connected as a group. To the extent boards can get individual members to connect over their governance role and the tasks they are performing, they can benefit from cohesion without opening themselves up completely to the social pressures discussed in this book.

This still does not get around the point that *social* cohesion is both good and bad for groups. The best boards can do is to facilitate an environment in which social connections are supported but do not become dominant in board process. Awareness of the deleterious effects of social cohesion is, of course, the first step, and board leaders and members alike must critically self-assess on this dimension.

Dissent, But Not Dissension

We have already explained the benefits of allowing and even encouraging dissent. However, it needs to be constructive dissent, leading to healthy debate. If the dissent becomes disruptive, personal, disrespectful, condescending, or disloyal, it is unproductive. It can lead to power struggles, resentment, withdrawal, and much wasted time.

One way to deal with this tension is to be explicit about dissent when it occurs. Boards must identify the point of conflict and even discuss whether or not the dissent is useful given a particular stage of discussion. The leader must be careful to be objective and attuned to the board when a discussion like this happens. Board members who raised constructive points of dissent should be encouraged and praised. An explicit commitment to effective *process* that is revisited on occasion can allow boards to have dissent while avoiding dissension.

Collectivist Feelings, But Not Too Much

On some of the best boards, the directors have the feeling of being part of a unified body—one that is working on collective tasks. The board is a team, and all members of the team share the goals. But these collectivist feelings make it more likely that individual board members will loaf. Board members might feel that they can leave some of the hard work to others or might feel that their contributions will not necessarily make a difference to the group outcome. Boards may address this tension by continually *framing* their work in the collective sense but occasionally using a process that highlights and requires individual contributions.

Psychological Safety, But With Accountability

It is important for board members to be able and willing to express their beliefs and feelings openly in board meetings. They should feel that it is safe to express their inner feelings and to disclose their mistakes. But board evaluations should also hold individual board members accountable for their failures or for not contributing. Loafing and surreptitious plotting should not be tolerated any more than overt mistakes.

A Strong Chair, But Not Too Strong

Board chairs, or lead independent directors, are responsible for effective board conduct. They must shape the board norms and culture. They play a primary role in setting the agenda and framing the issues. They pace the discussions, sometimes speeding them to decision conclusions and other times scheduling breaks to allow for further off-line contemplation. If needed, they can guide the deliberations to head off destructive conflict between board members. They may suggest committees to perform particular tasks or designate a devil's advocate to draw out differing perspectives on a particularly challenging issue.

But board chairs should govern, not rule. They must encourage each board member to express their ideas in the search for the best group decision. And, of course, they should not use their power inappropriately, such as by using deceptive or bullying tactics, to further their own personal ends. This is a fine line that is easily crossed even by the most well-intentioned board leaders. To avoid this, the board leader should check in regularly and formally with some other designated member of the board who may provide group feedback.

Some Limits on the CEO's Power, But Not Too Many

While ostensibly CEOs report to the board, they actually have enormous power *over* the board. CEOs have direct authority over the company's staff resources and information, and because they work for the company full time, they have a knowledge advantage. CEOs who also serve as the board chair exert considerable influence on the board agenda and style of deliberations. The other board members must rein in the CEO's power to ensure that the board is not blind to his or her failures and limitations, that it is not being unduly influenced by the CEO's biases, and that overall it is conducting its affairs properly.

But boards can easily overstep their oversight role and start taking on some of the roles that are best left to management. A recent Harvard report on boardroom dynamics, although sharply critical of overbearing CEOs, argues that when a board "expresses skepticism about management's proposals, it undermines the supportive climate that is important for its CEO to succeed"—as if the corner office were kindergarten.[5] There is a fine line between oversight and direct management, or even micromanagement, and the place to draw that line changes over time, such as in moments of crisis or even lagging performance.

Many experts, rating agencies, and increasingly, lawmakers recommend that the roles of the CEO and board chair should be split to limit the CEO's power. But that advice is not always correct either. Some boards operate very effectively with direction provided by a lead independent director. And splitting the CEO and board leadership roles increases the potential for conflict between the CEO and the board, and that type of conflict is usually dysfunctional.

Routines Versus Breaking Up the Routines

Like all people, board members are creatures of habit, and board meetings, agendas, timetables, and processes typically follow regularized patterns. Having these regular routines reduces anxiety and stress. Personal calendars are easier to organize, and with a regular routine, things happen as they are expected to happen. If they are well designed, board routines also allow the board to operate efficiently.

But routines also have their dark side. The exact characteristic that allows routines to reduce board member anxiety—predictability—is the feature that causes routines to discourage awareness of and responses to new environmental cues. Boards might be following their normal routine and miss some new issues that should be discussed. A possible solution to this tension is to change the calendars, processes, and routines periodically to unfreeze the board members' thinking processes.

Avoiding or Minimizing the Most Serious Pathologies

We concluded each of the prior chapters with a list of steps that should be taken to minimize the damage that could be caused by the particular decision-making pathology discussed in that chapter. In this section, we highlight three particularly important features of good board functioning that can reduce the harmful effects of multiple pathologies: creating constructive dissent, getting the right board composition, and committing to meaningful board evaluations.

Creating Constructive Dissent

The conduct of board meetings—how discussion is managed, how information is shared, and how dissent is incorporated—is critically important to the board's effectiveness. Of course, the leader of the board, as the manager of this process, becomes a centrally important figure. Board chairs must establish good decision-making processes; this requires group norms that encourage and expect participation from every board member and the constructive use of dissent.

If every member cannot participate in meetings of the full board—perhaps because time is too short, topics too many, or the board too large—then some issues should be delegated to smaller work units (committees, either standing or temporary) where individual contributions (and loafing) are more easily recognizable. Directors must know what they and others contribute uniquely to the board and that their participation can be recognized and evaluated.

Encouraging dissent is a bit trickier. The board leader must support a board culture that encourages the expressions of minority opinions. Other board members must cooperate and support those norms. Dissent should be a board member's obligation and a regularly occurring and accepted part of the group process. Dissent can sometimes be encouraged by appointing a devil's advocate, or alternatively, an outsider can be brought in to some board meetings to play the devil's advocate role. Having a devil's advocate speak out is not the same as encouraging true dissent. However, it can be useful both because it allows different information sets and viewpoints to surface and because it often provides less emotional paths for moving through situations of conflict.

Dissent is also more likely to occur in longer meetings that allow more time for discussion. Longer discussions allow for the possibility of moving beyond shared information, which is usually discussed first. Board members who are looking at their watches, perhaps worried about whether they will be able to catch their plane, are not likely to bring up points of dissent, and they are not likely to be open to points of dissent brought up by others. The question of time is a sensitive one for many board members who feel pressed and hurried, even to make space for a few extra hours. However, it is reasonable, given what we know about group dynamics, to question in a fundamental

way whether the current typical duration and frequency of board meetings is enough.

Being explicit about time norms and adhering to them diligently can
free up board members to trust the board's process and explore paths of
discussion they otherwise would not. A norm of "we'll get out of here
as soon as we're done" is different from "we'll be leaving here at five
no matter what." When board members sense that their time is being
respected—that is, they are not being bombarded with needless management presentations and "performances" or getting 150-page board books
of useless information—they are more apt to be committed to the time
they give. One board we observed was extremely diligent about respect-
ing board member time, requiring each management report to be nar-
rowed down to one page of text and virtually assuring board members
of an "on-time departure" even if it meant postponing a discussion to
a future meeting. This allowed them to express meaningful dissent and
further kept them from checking their watches at every juncture. Most
board members we know are not averse to spending time on board work.
They simply want their time to be used constructively.

Ultimately, directors—or the members of any small group—need to
figure out how to have what has been called "a good fight."[6] They need to
recognize that dissent does not mean dissension. Studies have found that
the most successful companies have leadership teams that actively encourage conflict, recognizing that people can reach an intelligent collective decision even when they disagree. Alfred Sloan, who ran GM from 1923 to
1956, was on to something when he said at a meeting,

> Gentlemen, I take it that we are all in complete agreement on the
> decision here. Then, I propose that we postpone further discus-
> sion of this matter until our next meeting to give ourselves time
> to develop disagreement and perhaps gain some understanding of
> what the decision is all about.[7]

In board settings, the absence of conflict does not necessarily indicate
agreement. It could indicate confusion, timidity, acquiescence, or apathy.

Dissent, as we have discussed in this book, helps reduce destructive
conformity, the shared information bias, and the pluralistic ignorance

problem. It can also stimulate critical and creative thinking. The highest performing companies have at least some nonconformist board members who regard dissent as an obligation and who consider no subject to be undiscussable.[8] CEOs, chairs, lead directors, and boards in general need to demonstrate through their actions that they understand the difference between dissent and disloyalty.[9]

Sometimes group decision aids can be helpful. Individual debriefings with the chair before the board meeting and blind votes, processes, or both that allow individuals to make their contributions silently—such as in writing, electronically, or confidentially to an outside consultant interviewer—can have any of many benefits. These aids can avoid much of the self-censoring caused by evaluation apprehension. They can also improve productivity because they allow individuals to contribute their ideas without interruption. They can reduce the extreme persuasiveness of the chair or one board member. And, finally, they can eliminate the social comparisons that can lead to group polarization.

Board Composition

Board composition has not been a primary focus of this book. It is obvious that having the right-sized board and a mix of the right people on the board is critically important. These board qualities are at least as important as formal structures and procedures. We began this book with the assumption that the board is not too small and not too large, and comprises highly knowledgeable, experienced board members, none with destructive personalities, who collectively have the right mix of needed skills. But considering the group pathologies that we have discussed leads us to a more developed understanding of board composition and particularly what qualities individual board members must have to enable board effectiveness. Good board composition requires more than knowledge and expertise.

Obviously the single most important component of the board is the leader, either a chair or a lead independent director. This is implicit in many of the previous discussions. Among other things, board leaders should be unbiased and have good facilitation skills. They must understand the subtleties of group dynamics and know how to create effective norms.

Selection of a good mix of individual board members is also important. Board vigilance is among the most important board qualities.[10] To ensure vigilance, rather than passivity, and to counter the tendencies for social loafing, all individual board members should have inherent interest in the industry and the issues being faced. The board members should also have high confidence but not to the point where it reaches what could be called arrogance. Confident board members are more willing to take a stand against the collective judgment of the group, or at least a dominant coalition of the group. Arrogance, or an extremely high sense of self-efficacy, on the other hand, makes board members less tolerant of new ideas.

As a group, the board should be diverse. Having too many directors with the same backgrounds, skills, and orientation can create blinders and lead to groupthink. It can also lead to productivity losses if the directors are prone to talk about less important technical details among themselves. Also, importantly, board diversity means having diversity in perceptions, attitudes, and philosophies. These qualities reflect less visible kinds of diversity, which are often overlooked but are extremely important. These personal qualities might be related to traits that are easier to observe, such as gender, race, and social and educational background, but the direct relationship is not apparent in all cases. Having this kind of diversity of worldview and philosophy provides a broader set of perspectives, which, in turn, reduces the potential for mindless conformity. Diversity in expertise is also important as it allows boards to reduce the chance of group polarization; instead, basing decisions on facts and experience. Group diversity also reduces the social cohesion on a board, making a culture of open dissent easier to create. Boards that are not diverse in these many ways should encourage some board member turnover.

Board Evaluations

No group learns without feedback—comparisons of actual performance with performance expectations. Feedback is an important and expected part of management process. But formal feedback processes are far less well engrained at the board level than they are in the management ranks; perhaps no group gets less feedback than boards of directors.

There are reasons for the common lack of board evaluative feedback, of course; board evaluations take time, and they are notoriously difficult to do. With internal, peer evaluations, board members are typically reluctant to criticize their fellow directors. Criticism from within can destroy the sense of teamwork that sustains much board activity, and the source of harsh evaluations is often not difficult to infer, particularly on smaller boards. The effectiveness of outside evaluations is limited because the outsiders cannot be well informed. They cannot understand the full context in which the board operates and will operate, and they can observe only a small sample of board deliberations and actions, if they observe them at all. And many boards are concerned about legal risks because the information that is gathered during evaluation processes is potentially discoverable. Too many times board evaluations are treated as an annoying necessity that becomes a meaningless, mechanical process of filling in boxes on a checklist.

Still, meaningful board evaluations must be done. There is considerable evidence that good evaluations are value adding; they improve board, and hence corporate, performance.[11] They are critically important for a number of reasons. First, the evaluations must be done in comparison with some performance standards. The mere development and communication of the standards can clarify what the board hopes to achieve—that is, how it expects to contribute to the overall effectiveness of the organization. The standards define roles, responsibilities, and expectations and, consequently, shape behavior in desirable ways. The performance standards should consider explicitly each of the factors toward which we have directed attention in this book. The evaluation processes can serve as a valuable training exercise for new directors who might only be able to participate as outside observers in their first year. Second, good board evaluations must be done down to the level of individuals, to hold board members individually accountable. These evaluations help minimize the problem of social loafing (or free riding) as well as help board members learn how they can improve their performances. The evaluations should go beyond the element of quantity of contributions and address the quality of those contributions and the board dynamics as a whole. For example, board members should be evaluated on the extent to which they contribute to constructive debate, and board leaders should be evaluated on the extent to which they encourage constructive debate and contributions from all board members. The evaluations should compare actual performance against performance expectations in all these areas.

Third, the board evaluations can and should lead to specific improvements in the board's focus, organization, and processes. They can, for example, suggest areas of oversight or time wasting. They can provide the information necessary to confront poor-performing directors or board leaders. The result should be improved effectiveness and efficiency.

And, finally, board evaluations can improve board communications and culture. Done well, the evaluations should encourage a culture of open communication among board members and management. An enhanced culture should reduce both corporate risk and directors' personal risk, thus making the company more attractive to strategic partners, potential board candidates, and directors and officers' liability insurers.

There is no universally recognized best evaluation process that boards can use as a guide, but general recommendations are provided by a number of organizations, such as the National Association of Corporate Directors.[12] Actually, companies can and do use a variety of processes for collecting and analyzing information while preserving needed confidentiality. Some companies use paper evaluation forms. The data from those forms are summarized and fed back to the board by the board chair or lead independent director. Other companies use web-based evaluations. An example of a web-based instrument can be found at http://www .directorevaluation.com. Those data can be automatically summarized in report form for the board to consider. Some companies use outside facilitators to enhance the evaluation process. The outsiders can collect data from board members, such as through interviews, reviews of board policies and procedures, and perhaps even observations of board meetings. The outsiders typically gather more information than is possible with just the use of questionnaires, even those with open-ended questions. The outsiders can add both an objective viewpoint and their own ideas as to how what they observed compares with generally accepted best practice. The outsiders can also be used to help ensure follow-up in the improvement phase of the evaluation process. The feedback is not useful if it is not acted upon to improve board performance and the company's corporate governance system.

The evaluation approaches can be combined, of course. Some companies conduct surveys annually and bring in outsiders less frequently, perhaps every 3 years.

Board evaluations cannot be done once and then forgotten about; they should be done formally on a regular basis, at defined intervals, and less formally on an ongoing basis. The board must agree about the value of the evaluations and approach the task with enthusiasm. For self-evaluations, all board members must be prepared to answer important questions regarding, for example, board expectations; individuals' contributions, both desired and actual; and changes that should be made. This is yet another area where success depends heavily on the board leader, who must push directors to engage in the process in a serious and open manner. Leaders must ensure, for example, that the board members do not rate each other highly just to move through the process quickly and without confrontation. A board should be wary if the main conclusion from the evaluations is that no improvements are necessary.

Inherent Board Limitations

After reading the discussions in this and prior chapters, one might wonder how boards of directors (and other groups) ever reach rational, informed decisions. Can corporate governance be effectively provided by boards of directors? That is a valid question, one that should receive much more debate than it has. Certainly there are inherent limitations to what can be expected of groups of board members. There is no panacea. Many of the blind spots, biases, and other pathologies described in this book are nearly inevitable. Recognition of the potential problems is a necessary first step. Then steps such as those we have suggested can be taken to try to avoid or minimize some of the effects of the pathologies.

As a society, we must recognize that there are inherent limitations in what can be expected of corporate governance provided by groups of board members. No one should be shocked when corporate failures become public knowledge and are blamed at least in part on boards of directors who appear to be following all the best-practice guidelines, at least those suggested by the now-existing rating organizations. Such failures have occurred regularly in the past, and they will continue to occur in the future.

Does that mean that corporate governance should not be provided by board member groups? That certainly is not our conclusion. We think that there really is no alternative to providing corporate oversight by a group. No single individual can bring the time available, the breadth of talent, and the different perspectives necessary to provide an effective check on the ways in which management is directing and controlling the organization. The practical issue is how best to take advantage of the benefits the board provides while minimizing, as much as possible, the blind spots, biases, and other pathologies that can have such negative effects.

Regulators and society must understand these limitations and be realistic about what boards of directors can do. As they contemplate instituting other complementary forms of governance, oversight, and regulations, the blind spots of boards should be kept in mind. Overregulation of board behavior is almost certainly not the answer, and in fact it arguably exacerbates some of the problems we have been discussing by cutting into valuable discussion time, bogging directors down with largely meaningless and tedious activities, and generally causing them to become distanced from the actual business and intrinsic interest they have in being board members.

We aim our suggestions primarily at the population of board members who may gain insight into their own group processes and tendencies by considering the pathologies and blind spots we have identified. By acknowledging them and incorporating our suggestions, their boards can avoid many of the failures such as we have seen on repeated occasions throughout modern history.

Notes

Chapter 1

1. Leonhardt (2002).
2. Monks and Minow (2008).
3. Monks and Minow (2008).
4. National Association of Corporate Directors (2008), p. 5.
5. Daines, Gow, and Larcker (2008).
6. According to a study by The Corporate Library, the average board size is 9.2 members, with a range from 3 to 31.
7. Yermack (1996).
8. Brooks and Dunn (2009), p. 72.
9. Permanent Subcommittee on Investigations of the Committee on Governmental Affairs, U.S. Senate (2002).

Chapter 2

1. Karau and Williams (1993).
2. See Ingham, Levinger, Graves, and Pechham (1974).
3. Ingham, Levinger, Graves, and Pechham (1974).
4. Latané, Williams, and Harkins (1979).
5. Latané, Williams, and Harkins (1979).
6. Harkins and Jackson (1985); Harkins and Szymanski (1989).
7. Kerr (1983); Kerr and Bruun (1983).
8. Hardy and Crace (1991).
9. Karau and Williams (1993).
10. Karau and Williams (1993).
11. Hardy and Latané (1988).
12. Pick (2007).
13. Szymanski and Harkins (1987).
14. Deutsch and Gerard (1955).
15. Ono and Davis (1988).
16. Sherif (1936).
17. Asch (1951).
18. Asch (1951), p. 179.
19. Baron, Vandello, and Brunsman (1996).

Chapter 3

1. For example, Parisi and Smith (2005).
2. Nutt (2002); Arkes and Blumer (1985).
3. Arkes and Ayton (1999).
4. For example, Kerr and Tindale (2004); Stewart, Billings, and Stasser (1998).
5. Kerr and Tindale (2004); Postmes, Spears, and Cihangir (2001).
6. Wittenbaum, Hubbell, and Zuckerman (1999).
7. Stasser, Taylor, and Hanna (1989).
8. Kerr and Tindale (2004).
9. Stasser, Taylor, and Hanna (1989).
10. Wittenbaum (1998).
11. Winquist and Larson (1998).
12. Lam and Schaubroeck (2000).
13. Harvey (2001).
14. Harvey (2001), p. 18.
15. Westphal and Bednar (2005).
16. Miller, Monin, and Prentice (2000).
17. Westphal and Bednar (2005).
18. Halbesleben, Wheeler, and Buckley (2007).
19. Westphal and Bednar (2005).

Chapter 4

1. Stoner (1961).
2. Stoner (1961).
3. Moscovici and Zavalloni (1969); Myers and Lamm (1976).
4. Myers and Bishop (1971).
5. Festinger (1954).
6. Festinger (1954).
7. Burnstein (1982); Burnstein and Vinokur (1977).
8. Brown (1986).
9. Goethals and Zanna (1979).

Chapter 5

1. See Janis (1982); Whyte (1998).
2. Janis (1982), p. 9.
3. Jennings (2006), p. 168.
4. Asch (1951).
5. Baron (2005).
6. Baron (2005).

7. Hogg and Hains (1998).

8. Baron (2005).

9. Baron (2005).

10. Baron (2005), p. 243.

11. Baron (2005), p. 244.

12. Kirkpatrick (2000), p. 127.

13. Tripathi (2009).

14. Zarowin (2005), p. 109.

15. Marnet (2008).

Chapter 6

1. Gersick and Hackman (1990), p. 69.

2. Gersick and Hackman (1990), p. 65; National Transportation Safety Board (1982).

3. Bales (1950).

4. March and Simon (1958).

5. Meyer and Rowan (1977).

6. Nelson and Winter (1982).

7. Barley (1986).

8. Langer (1978).

9. Knicely (1983).

10. Langer (1989).

11. Gersick and Hackman (1990).

12. Khurana and Pick (2005).

13. Weiss and Ilgen (1985).

14. de Bono (1999).

Chapter 7

1. De Dreu and Weingart (2003).

2. Hackman and Morris (1975).

3. Saavedra, Earley, and Van Dyne (1993); Wall and Nolan (1986).

4. Gladstein (1984).

5. Amason and Schweiger (1994); Jehn (1995).

6. Jehn (1997); Nemeth (1986); Schultz-Hardt, Jochims, and Frey (2002).

7. De Dreu and Weingart (2003).

8. Jehn (1997); Jehn, Greer, Levine, and Szulanski (2008); Jehn and Mannix (2001).

9. Jehn, Greer, Levine, and Szulanski (2008).

10. Jehn (1994, 1995, 1997).

11. Simons and Peterson (2000).

12. Hollenbeck et al. (1995); Schultz-Hardt, Jochims, and Frey (2002); Schwenk (1990).

13. De Dreu and Weingart (2003).

14. De Dreu and Weingart (2003).

15. Jehn and Bendersky (2003).

16. Jehn, Greer, Levine, and Szulanski (2008).

17. Jehn, Greer, Levine, and Szulanski (2008).

18. Jehn, Greer, Levine, and Szulanski (2008).

19. Jehn (1997).

20. Pinkley (1990).

21. Jehn, Greer, Levine, and Szulanski (2008).

22. Jehn, Greer, Levine, and Szulanski (2008).

23. Jehn, Greer, Levine, and Szulanski (2008).

24. Lewin (1947).

25. Pelled, Eisenhardt, and Xin (1999).

26. Mooney, Holahan, and Amason (2007).

27. Sherif, Harvey, White, Hood, and Sherif (1961).

28. De Dreu and Van Vianen (2001).

29. Simons and Peterson (2000).

30. Dirks and Ferrin (2001).

31. Edmondson (1999).

32. Schwenk (1990).

33. Alper, Tjosvold, and Law (2000).

34. Lovelace, Shapiro, and Weingart (2001).

35. Tajfel and Turner (1986).

36. Goffman (1959).

Chapter 8

1. Huse (2007).

2. Russell (1938).

3. Pfeffer (1992).

4. Huse (2007).

5. Pettigrew and McNulty (1995), p. 865.

6. Yukl, Guinan, and Sottolano (1995).

7. Hill (1995), p. 256.

8. Westphal and Stern (2007).

9. Murray (2007).

10. Pearce and Zahra (1991).

11. Lorsch and MacIver (1989); Pettigrew and McNulty (1995).

12. Pettigrew and McNulty (1995).

13. Larcker, Richardson, and Tuna (2007).

14. Hill (1995).

15. Krantz (2002).
16. Securities and Exchange Commission (2003).
17. Krantz (2002).
18. Davis (1991).
19. Mizruchi (1996).
20. Morrill (1995).
21. Morrill (1995), pp. 263–265.
22. Eisenhardt and Bourgeois (1988).

Chapter 9

1. Kerr and Tindale (2004).
2. Steiner (1972).
3. Paulus, Dzindolet, Poletes, and Camacho (1993).
4. Diehl and Stroebe (1987).
5. Steiner (1972).
6. Mullen, Johnson, and Salas (1991).
7. Diehl and Stroebe (1987).
8. Diehl and Stroebe (1987).
9. Diehl and Stroebe (1991).
10. Dyer, Dyer, and Dyer (2007).
11. Moreland and Myaskovsky (2000).
12. Mullen, Johnson, and Salas (1991).
13. For example, Nijstad, Rietzschel, and Stroebe (2005); Nijstad, Stroebe, and Lodewijkx (2003); Valacich, Dennis, and Connolly (1994).
14. Mankins (2004).
15. Laughlin, Shupe, and Magley (2003).

Chapter 10

1. Rattner (2009).
2. Sharfman and Toll (2008); Sonnenfeld (2002).
3. Westphal (1998).
4. Dion (2000).
5. Sonnenfeld (2002).
6. Eisenhardt, Kahwajy, and Bourgeois (1997).
7. Quoted many times, including in Drucker (1967), p. 139.
8. Eisenhardt, Kahwajy, and Bourgeois (1997).
9. Sonnenfeld (2002).
10. Finkelstein, Hambrick, and Cannella (2008).
11. Keil, Nicholson, and Barclay (2005); Stybel and Peabody (2005).
12. National Association of Corporate Directors (2008).

References

Alper, S., Tjosvold, D., & Law, K. S. (2000). Conflict management, efficacy, and performance in organizational teams. *Personnel Psychology, 53*, 625–642.

Amason, A. C., & Schweiger, D. M. (1994). Resolving the paradox of conflict, strategic decision making and organizational performance. *International Journal of Conflict Management, 5*, 239–253.

Arkes, H. R., & Ayton, P. (1999). The sunk cost and Concorde effects: Are humans less rational than lower animals? *Psychological Bulletin, 125*, 591–600.

Arkes, H. R., & Blumer, C. (1985). The psychology of sunk cost. *Organizational Behavior and Human Decision Processes, 35*, 124–140.

Asch, S. E. (1951). Effects of group pressure upon the modification and distortion of judgment. In H. Guetzkow (Ed.), *Groups, leadership and men* (pp. 177–190). Pittsburgh, PA: Carnegie Press.

Bales, R. F. (1950). *Interaction process analysis: A method for the study of small groups*. Cambridge, MA: Addison-Wesley.

Barley, S. R. (1986). Technology as an occasion for structuring: Evidence from observations of CT scanners and the social order of radiology departments. *Administrative Science Quarterly, 31*(1), 78–108.

Baron, R. S. (2005). So right it's wrong: Groupthink and the ubiquitous nature of polarized group decision making. In M. P. Zanna (Ed.), *Advances in experimental social psychology* (Vol. 37, pp. 219–253). San Diego, CA: Elsevier.

Baron, R. S., Vandello, J. A., & Brunsman, B. (1996). The forgotten variable in conformity research: Impact of task importance on social influence. *Journal of Personality and Social Psychology, 71*(5), 915–927.

Brooks, L. J., & Dunn, P. (2009). *Business & professional ethics for directors, executives & accountants* (5th ed.). Mason, OH: Southwestern.

Brown, R. (1986). *Social psychology*. New York, NY: The Free Press.

Burnstein, E. (1982). Persuasion as argument processing. In J. H. Davis & G. Stocher-Kreichgauer (Eds.), *Contemporary problems in group decision-making* (pp. 103–124). New York, NY: Academic Press.

Burnstein, E., & Vinokur, A. (1977). Persuasive argumentation and social comparison as determinants of attitude polarization. *Journal of Experimental Social Psychology, 13*(4), 315–332.

Daines, R., Gow, I., & Larcker, D. (2008). Rating the ratings: How good are commercial governance ratings? Unpublished working paper, Stanford University, Palo Alto, CA.

Davis, G. F. (1991). Agents without principles? The spread of the poison pill through the intercorporate network. *Administrative Science Quarterly, 36,* 583–613.

de Bono, E. (1999). *Six thinking hats.* New York, NY: Back Bay.

De Dreu, C. K. W., & Van Vianen, A. E. M. (2001). Managing relationship conflict and the effectiveness of organizational teams. *Journal of Organizational Behavior, 22*(3), 309–328.

De Dreu, C. K. W., & Weingart, L. R. (2003). Task versus relationship conflict, team performance, team member satisfaction: A meta-analysis. *Journal of Applied Psychology, 88,* 741–749.

Deutsch, M., & Gerard, H. (1955). A study of normative and informational social influences on individual judgment. *Journal of Abnormal and Social Psychology, 51,* 629–636.

Diehl, M., & Stroebe, W. (1987). Productivity loss in brainstorming groups: Toward the solution of a riddle. *Journal of Personality and Social Psychology, 53*(3), 497–509.

Diehl, M., & Stroebe, W. (1991). Productivity loss in idea-generating groups: Tracking down the blocking effect. *Journal of Personality and Social Psychology, 61*(3), 392–403.

Dion, K. L. (2000). Group cohesion: From "field of forces" to multidimensional construct. *Group Dynamics: Theory, Research, and Practice, 4*(1), 7–26.

Dirks, K. T., & Ferrin, D. L. (2001). The role of trust in organizational settings. *Organization Science, 12*(4), 450–467.

Drucker, P. F. (1967). *The effective executive.* Burlington, MA: Butterworth-Heinemann.

Dyer, W. G., Dyer, W. G., Jr., & Dyer, J. H. (2007). *Team building: Proven strategies for improving team performance* (4th ed.). San Francisco, CA: Jossey-Bass.

Edmondson, A. (1999). Psychological safety and learning in work teams. *Administrative Science Quarterly, 44,* 350–383.

Eisenhardt, K., & Bourgeois, L. J. (1988). Politics of strategic decision making in high velocity environments: Toward a mid-range theory. *Academy of Management Journal, 31,* 737–770.

Eisenhardt, K. M., Kahwajy, J. L., & Bourgeois, L. J., III. (1997, July–August). How management teams can have a good fight. *Harvard Business Review,* pp. 1–9.

Festinger, L. (1954). A theory of social comparison processes. *Human Relations, 7,* 117–140.

Finkelstein, S., Hambrick, D. C., & Cannella, A. (2008). *Strategic leadership: Theory and research on executives, top management teams, and boards.* Oxford, England: Oxford University Press.

Gersick, C. J. G., & Hackman, J. R. (1990). Habitual routines in task-performing teams. *Organizational Behavior and Human Decision Processes, 47*, 65–97.

Gladstein, D. L. (1984). Groups in context: A model of task group effectiveness. *Administrative Science Quarterly, 29*, 499–517.

Goethals, G. R., & Zanna, M. P. (1979). The role of social comparison in choice shifts. *Journal of Personality and Social Psychology, 37*(9), 1469–1476.

Goffman, E. (1959). *The presentation of self in everyday life.* Garden City, NY: Doubleday.

Hackman, J. R., & Morris, C. G. (1975). Group tasks, group interaction process, and group performance effectiveness: A review and proposed integration. In L. Berkowitz (Ed.), *Advances in experimental social psychology* (pp. 45–99). New York, NY: Academic Press.

Halbesleben, J. R. B., Wheeler, A. R., & Buckley, M. R. (2007). Understanding pluralistic ignorance in organizations: Application and theory. *Journal of Managerial Psychology, 22*(1), 65–83.

Hardy, C. J., & Crace, R. K. (1991). The effects of task structure and teammate competence on social loafing. *Journal of Sport and Exercise Psychology, 13*, 372–381.

Hardy, C. J., & Latané, B. (1988). Social loafing in cheerleaders: Effects of team membership and competition. *Journal of Sport and Exercise Psychology, 10*, 109–114.

Harkins, S. G., & Jackson, J. M. (1985). The role of evaluation in eliminating social loafing. *Personality and Social Psychology, 11*, 575–584.

Harkins, S. G., & Szymanski, K. (1989). Social loafing and group evaluation. *Journal of Personality and Social Psychology, 56*, 934–941.

Harvey, J. B. (2001). The Abilene paradox: The management of agreement. *Organizational Dynamics, 55*(2), 17–43.

Hill, S. (1995). The social organization of boards of directors. *British Journal of Sociology, 46*(2), 245–278.

Hogg, M. A., & Hains, S. C. (1998). Friendship and group identification: A new look at the role of cohesiveness in groupthink. *European Journal of Social Psychology, 28*, 323–341.

Hollenbeck, J. R., Ilgen, D. R., Sego, D. J., Hedlund, J., Major, D. A., & Phillips, J. (1995). Multilevel theory of team decision making: Decision performance in teams incorporating distributed expertise. *Journal of Applied Psychology, 80*, 292–3 16.

Huse, M. (2007). *Boards, governance and value creation.* Cambridge, England: Cambridge University Press.

Ingham, A. G., Levinger, G., Graves, J., & Pechham, V. (1974). The Ringelmann effect: Studies of group size and group performance. *Journal of Experimental Social Psychology, 10*, 371–384.

Janis, I. L. (1982). *Victims of groupthink: A psychological study of foreign-policy decisions and fiascos.* Boston, MA: Houghton Mifflin.

Jehn, K. A. (1994). Enhancing effectiveness: An investigation of advantages and disadvantages of value-based intragroup conflict. *International Journal of Conflict Management, 5*(3), 223–23 8.

Jehn, K. A. (1995). A multimethod examination of the benefits and detriments of intragroup conflict. *Administrative Science Quarterly, 40*, 256–282.

Jehn, K. A. (1997). A qualitative analysis of conflict types and dimensions in organizational groups. *Administrative Science Quarterly, 42*, 530–557.

Jehn, K. A., & Bendersky, C. (2003). Intragroup conflict in organizations: A contingency perspective on the conflict–outcome relationship. *Research in Organizational Behavior, 25*, 187–243.

Jehn, K. A., Greer, L., Levine, S., & Szulanski, G. (2008). The effects of conflict types, dimensions, and emergent states on group outcomes. *Group Decision and Negotiation, 17*(6), 465–495.

Jehn, K. A., & Mannix, E. (2001). The dynamic nature of conflict: A longitudinal study of intragroup conflict and group performance. *Academy of Management Journal, 44*(2), 238–251.

Jennings, M. M. (2006). *The seven signs of ethical collapse.* New York, NY: St. Martin's Press.

Karau, S. J., & Williams, K. D. (1993). Social loafing: A meta-analytic review and theoretical integration. *Journal of Personality and Social Psychology, 65*(4), 681–706.

Kiel, G. C., Nicholson, G., & Barclay, M. A. (2005) *Board, director and CEO evaluation.* Sydney, New South Wales, Australia: McGraw-Hill.

Kerr, N. L. (1983). Motivation losses in small groups: A social dilemma analysis. *Journal of Personality and Social Psychology, 45*, 819–828.

Kerr, N. L., & Bruun, S. (1983). The dispensability of member effort and group motivation losses: Free rider effects. *Journal of Personality and Social Psychology, 44*, 78–94.

Kerr, N. L., & Tindale, S. R. (2004). Group performance and decision making. *Annual Review of Psychology, 55*(22), 623–655.

Khurana, R., & Pick, K. (2005). The social nature of boards. *Brooklyn Law Review, 70*(4), 1259–1285.

Kirkpatrick, D. (2000, January 24). Enron takes its pipeline to the net. *Fortune.*

Knicely, A. S. (1983). *A study of the effect of job change in simulated organizations on work habits.* Unpublished master's thesis, Purdue University, West Lafayette, IN.

Krantz, M. (2002, November 24). Web of board members ties together corporate America. *USA Today*.

Lam, S. K., & Schaubroeck, J. (2000). Improving group decisions by better pooling information: A comparative advantage of group decision support systems. *Journal of Applied Psychology, 85*, 565–573.

Langer, E. J. (1978). Rethinking the role of thought in social interactions. In J. H. Harvey, W. J. Ickes, & R. F. Kidd (Eds.), *New directions in attribution theory* (Vol. 2, 3rd ed., pp. 35–58). Hillsdale, NJ: Erlbaum.

Langer, E. J. (1989). *Mindfulness*. Reading, MA: Addison-Wesley.

Larcker, D. F., Richardson, S. A., & Tuna, I. (2007). Corporate governance, accounting outcomes, and organizational performance. *The Accounting Review, 82*(4), 963–1008.

Latané, B., Williams, K., & Harkins, S. (1979). Many hands make light the work: The causes and consequences of social loafing. *Journal of Personality and Social Psychology, 37*(6), 822–832.

Laughlin, P. R., Shupe, E., & Magley, V. J. (2003). Effectiveness of positive hypothesis testing for cooperative groups. *Organizational Behavioral and Human Decision Processes, 73*, 27–38.

Leonhardt, D. (2002, June 9). Watch it: If you cheat, they'll throw you money! *New York Times*, p. 31.

Lewin, K. (1947). Frontiers in group dynamics: Concepts, method and reality in social science, social equilibria and social change. *Human Relations, 1*, 5–41.

Lorsch, J. W., & MacIver, E. (1989). *Pawns and potentates: The reality of America's corporate boards*. Boston, MA: Harvard Business School Press.

Lovelace, K., Shapiro, D. L., & Weingart, L. R. (2001). Maximizing cross-functional new product teams' innovativeness and constraint adherence: A conflict communications perspective. *Academy of Management Journal, 44*, 779–783.

Mankins, M. C. (2004, September). Stop wasting valuable time. *Harvard Business Review*, pp. 58–65.

March, J. G., & Simon, H. A. (1958). *Organizations*. New York, NY: Wiley.

Marnet, O. (2008). *Behaviour and rationality in corporate governance*. London: Routledge.

Meyer, J. W., & Rowan, B. (1977). Institutionalized organizations: Formal structure as myth and ceremony. *American Journal of Sociology, 83*, 340–363.

Miller, D. T., Monin, M., & Prentice, D. A. (2000). Pluralistic ignorance and inconsistency between private and public behaviors. In D. J. Terry & M. A. Hogg (Eds.), *Attitudes, behavior and social context: The role of norms and group membership* (pp. 95–113). Mahwah, NJ: Erlbaum.

Mizruchi, M. (1996). What do interlocks do? An analysis, critique, and assessment of research on interlocking directorates. *Annual Review of Sociology, 22,* 271–298.

Monks, R. A. G., & Minow, N. (2008). *Corporate governance* (4th ed.). Chichester, West Sussex, England: Wiley.

Mooney, A. C., Holahan, P. J., & Amason, A. C. (2007). Don't take it personally: Exploring cognitive conflict as a mediator of affective conflict. *Journal of Management Studies, 44*(5), 733–75 8.

Moreland, R. L., & Myaskovsky, L. (2000). Exploring the performance benefits of group training: Transactive memory or improved communication? *Organizational Behavior and Human Decision Processes, 82*(1), 117–133.

Morrill, C. (1995). *The executive way.* Chicago, IL: University of Chicago Press.

Moscovici, S., & Zavalloni, M. (1969). The group as a polarizer of attitudes. *Journal of Personality and Social Psychology, 12,* 125–135.

Mullen, B., Johnson, C., & Salas, E. (1991). Productivity loss in brainstorming groups: A meta-analytic integration. *Basic and Applied Psychology, 12,* 2–23.

Murray, A. (2007). *Revolt in the boardroom: The new rules of power in corporate America.* New York, NY: Collins.

Myers, D. G., & Bishop, G. D. (1971). The enhancement of dominant attitudes in group discussion. *Journal of Personality and Social Psychology, 20,* 386–391.

Myers, D. G., & Lamm, H. (1976). The group polarization phenomenon. *Psychological Bulletin, 83,* 602–627.

National Association of Corporate Directors (NACD). (2008, October 16). *Key agreed principles to strengthen corporate governance for U.S. publicly traded companies.* Washington, DC: Author.

National Transportation Safety Board (NTSB). (1982, August 10). *Aircraft accident report* (AAR Publication No. 82-08).

Nelson, S. G., & Winter, R. R. (1982). *An evolutionary theory of economic change.* Cambridge, MA: Harvard University Press.

Nemeth, C. J. (1986). Differential contributions of majority and minority influence processes. *Psychological Review, 93,* 10–20.

Nijstad, B. A., Rietzschel, E. F., & Stroebe, W. (2005). Four principles of group creativity. In L. Thompson & H.-S. Choi (Eds.), *Creativity and innovation in organizational teams* (pp. 161–179). Hillsdale, NJ: Erlbaum.

Nijstad, B. A., Stroebe, W., & Lodewijkx, H. F. M. (2003). Cognitive stimulation and interference in groups: Exposure effects in an idea generation task. *Journal of Experimental Social Psychology, 39,* 531–548.

Nutt, P. C. (2002). *Why decisions fail: Avoiding the blunders and traps that lead to debacles.* San Francisco, CA: Berrett-Koehler.

Ono, K., & Davis, J. H. (1988). Individual judgment and group interaction: A variable perspective approach. *Organizational Behavior and Human Decision Processes, 41*(2), 211–232.

Parisi, F., & Smith, V. L. (2005). *The law and economics of irrational behavior.* Palo Alto, CA: Stanford University Press.

Paulus, P. B., Dzindolet, M. T., Poletes, G., & Camacho, L. M. (1993). Perceptions of performance in group brainstorming: The illusion of group productivity. *Personality and Social Psychology, 64,* 575–586.

Pearce, J. A., II, & Zahra, S. A. (1991). The relative power of CEOs and boards of directors: Associations with corporate performance. *Strategic Management Journal, 12,* 135–153.

Pelled, L. H., Eisenhardt, K. M., & Xin, K. R. (1999). Exploring the black box: An analysis of work group diversity, conflict, and performance. *Administrative Science Quarterly, 44*(1), 1–28.

Permanent Subcommittee on Investigations of the Committee on Governmental Affairs, U.S. Senate. (2002, July 8). *The role of the board of directors in Enron's collapse.* Washington, DC: U.S. Government Printing Office.

Pettigrew, A., & McNulty, T. (1995). Power and influence in and around the boardroom. *Human Relations, 48*(8), 845–873.

Pfeffer, J. (1992). *Managing with power.* Boston, MA: Harvard Business School Press.

Pick, K. (2007). *Around the boardroom table: Interactional aspects of governance.* Unpublished doctoral dissertation, Harvard Business School, Boston, MA.

Pinkley, R. (1990). Dimensions of the conflict frame: Disputant interpretations of conflict. *Journal of Applied Psychology, 75,* 117–128.

Postmes, T., Spears, R., & Cihangir, S. (2001). Quality of decision making and group norms. *Journal of Personality and Social Psychology, 80,* 918–930.

Rattner, S. (2009, October 21). The auto bailout: How we did it. *Fortune.*

Russell, B. (1938). *Power: A social analysis.* New York, NY: Norton.

Saavedra, R., Earley, P. C., & Van Dyne, L. (1993). Complex interdependence in task-performing groups. *Journal of Applied Psychology, 78*(1), 61–72.

Schultz-Hardt, S. M., Jochims, M., & Frey, D. (2002). Productive conflict in group decision-making: Genuine and contrived dissent as strategies to counteract biased information seeking. *Organizational Behavior and Human Decision Processes, 88,* 563–586.

Schwenk, C. R. (1990). Effect of devil's advocacy and dialectical inquiry on decision making: A meta-analysis. *Organizational Behavior and Human Decision Processes, 47,* 161–176.

Securities and Exchange Commission. (2003, April 28). *Litigation release* (No. 18111).

Sharfman, B. S., & Toll, S. J. (2008). Dysfunctional deference and board composition: Lessons from Enron. *Northwestern University Law Review Colloquy, 103*, 153–162.

Sherif, M. (1936). *The psychology of social norms.* New York, NY: Harper.

Sherif, M., Harvey, O. J., White, B. J., Hood, W. R., & Sherif, C. W. (1961). *Intergroup conflict and cooperation: The robbers cave experiment.* Norman, OK: Institute of Social Relations.

Simons, T., & Peterson, R. (2000). Task conflict and relationship conflict in top management teams: The pivotal role of intragroup trust. *Journal of Applied Psychology, 85*, 102–111.

Sonnenfeld, J. A. (2002, September). What makes great boards great. *Harvard Business Review*, pp. 2–10.

Stasser, G., Taylor, L. A., & Hanna, C. (1989). Information sampling of structured and unstructured discussions of three and six person groups. *Journal of Personality and Social Psychology, 57*, 67–78.

Steiner, I. D. (1972). *Group process and productivity.* New York, NY: Academic Press.

Stewart, D. D., Billings, R. S., & Stasser, G. (1998). Accountability and the discussion of unshared, critical information in decision-making groups. *Group Dynamics: Theory, Research, and Practice, 2*, 18–23.

Stoner, J. A. F. (1961). *Comparison of individual and group decisions involving risk.* Unpublished master's thesis, Massachusetts Institute of Technology, School of Industrial Management.

Stybel, L. J., & Peabody, M. (2005). How should board directors evaluate themselves? *MIT Sloan Management Review, 47*(1), 67–72.

Szymanski, K., & Harkins, S. G. (1987). Social loafing and self-evaluation with a social standard. *Journal of Personality and Social Psychology, 53*(5), 891–897.

Tajfel, H., & Turner, J. C. (1986). The social identity theory of intergroup behavior. In S. Worchel & W. G. Austin (Eds.), *Psychology of intergroup relations* (pp. 7–24). Chicago, IL: Nelson-Hall.

Tripathi, S. (2009, January 9). India faces an "Enron moment." *Wall Street Journal.*

Valacich, J. S., Dennis, A. R., & Connolly, T. (1994). Idea generation in computer-based groups: A new ending to an old story. *Organizational Behavior and Human Decision Processes, 7*(3), 448–467.

Wall, V. D., & Nolan, L. L. (1986). Perceptions of inequity, satisfaction, and conflict in task-oriented groups. *Human Relations, 39*(11), 1033–1051.

Weiss, H. M., & Ilgen, D. R. (1985). Routinized behavior in organizations. *Journal of Behavioral Economics, 14*, 57–67.

Westphal, J. D. (1998). Board games: How CEOs adapt to increases in structural board independence from management. *Administrative Science Quarterly, 43,* 511–537.

Westphal, J. D., & Bednar, K. K. (2005). Pluralistic ignorance in corporate boards and firms' strategic persistence in response to low firm performance. *Administrative Science Quarterly, 50,* 262–298.

Westphal, J. D., & Stern, I. (2007). Flattery will get you everywhere (especially if you are a male Caucasian): How ingratiation, boardroom behavior, and demographic minority status affect additional board appointments at U.S. companies. *Academy of Management Journal, 50*(2), 267–288.

Whyte, G. (1998). Recasting Janis's groupthink model: The key role of collective efficacy in decision fiascoes. *Organizational Behavior and Human Decision Processes, 73,* 185–209.

Winquist, J. R., & Larson, J. R., Jr. (1998). Information pooling: When it impacts group decision making. *Journal of Personality and Social Psychology, 74,* 371–377.

Wittenbaum, G. M. (1998). Information sampling in decision-making groups: The impact of members' task-relevant status. *Small Group Research, 29,* 57–84.

Wittenbaum, G. M., Hubbell, A. P., & Zuckerman, C. (1999). Mutual enhancement: Toward an understanding of collective preference for shared information. *Journal of Personality and Social Psychology, 77,* 967–978.

Yermack, D. (1996). Higher market valuation of companies with a small board of directors. *Journal of Financial Economics, 40,* 185–211.

Yukl, G., Guinan, P. J., & Sottolano, D. (1995). Influence tactics used for different objectives with subordinates, peers, and superiors. *Group & Organization Management, 20*(3), 272–296.

Zarowin, S. (2005). Golden business ideas. *Journal of Accountancy, 200*(1), 109.

Index